Invitations to Psychology

General Editor:

Professor Windy Dryden
Goldsmiths' College, University of London

Other titles in this series

Invitation to Personal Construct Psychology
Viven Burr and Trevor Butt

Invitation to Person-Centred Psychology
Tony Merry

To the Staff of QuickSnack, Euston.
Thank you for sustaining me with my regular order of tea with extra milk. Special thanks to Leroy and Ola.

Invitation to Rational-Emotive Psychology

Windy Dryden

Whurr Publishers Ltd
London

© 1994 Whurr Publishers Ltd

First published 1994 by
Whurr Publishers Ltd
19B Compton Terrace, London N1 2UN, England

All rights reserved. No part of this publication may be reproduced, stored in a retrieval system, or transmitted in any form or by any means, electronic, mechanical, photocopying, recording or otherwise, without the prior permission of Whurr Publishers Limited.

This publication is sold subject to the conditions that it shall not, by way of trade or otherwise, be lent, resold, hired out, or otherwise circulated without the publisher's prior consent in any form of binding or cover other than that in which it is published and without a similar condition including this condition being imposed upon any subsequent purchaser.

British Library Cataloguing-in-Publication Data
A catalogue record for this book is available from the
British Library

ISBN 1-897635-51-6

Printed and bound in the UK by Athenaeum Press Ltd, Newcastle upon Tyne

Contents

Chapter 1   1
Introduction

Chapter 2   9
Activating events

Chapter 3   17
Beliefs

Chapter 4   39
ABC's and the principle of emotional responsibility

Chapter 5   51
Emotions

Chapter 6   63
Behaviour

Chapter 7   81
Common emotional problems

Chapter 8   111
Complex relationships among the ABC's of rational-emotive psychology

Suggestions for futher reading

References   127

Index   129

Chapter 1
Introduction

In this opening chapter I introduce rational–emotive psychology (REP), give a brief history of the development of this approach, explain what is meant by the terms 'rational' and 'emotive' as they are used in REP, and outline the ABC framework which is at the core of REP.

What is rational–emotive psychology?

Rational–emotive psychology is an approach to psychology which considers the influence that people's beliefs (both rational and irrational), emotions and behaviours have on their psychological well-being.

In fact, there is no separate approach to the psychology known as rational–emotive psychology which specifically seeks to account for all things human. When speaking of REP I mean an approach to psychology that seeks, in a fairly unique way, to shed light on certain aspects of what it means to be human. As rational–emotive psychology, if we can speak of such a term, is derived from an approach to counselling and psychotherapy currently known as rational emotive behaviour therapy (REBT), it will come as no surprise to learn that the focus of REP is on psychological disturbance, psychological health and therapeutic change. As this has been the focus of REP, in this book I concentrate on these three areas of human functioning.

This does not mean that rational–emotive principles have not been applied to other areas of psychology. They have. For example, Albert Ellis (1978) – the founder of REBT – wrote a chapter on the rational–emotive approach to personality. He wrote this somewhat reluctantly, however, and acknowledged that he was going beyond the range of convenience of his theoretical ideas. As such, I only allude to what REP has to say about human personality.

I do not apologise for the somewhat restricted focus of this book. It is important to recognise what an approach to psychology both does and does not seek to explain. By this, I am not implying that REP cannot explain human learning and child development – to name two areas with which psychologists are centrally concerned – but stressing that to date no-one has applied rational–emotive principles to these areas in a systematic manner.

I shall not, however, start such an ambitious project in this book. Rather, as the title of the book makes clear, and in keeping with the focus of other books in this series, I invite you to consider the spirit and flavour of rational–emotive psychology, and to see what it has to offer in helping you to understand yourself and others. This is not a self-help book and, although I shall discuss how people who experience certain distressing emotions such as anxiety, anger and guilt can free themselves from these disabling feelings, I shall not be spelling out a step-by-step, self-help guide to personal change. No doubt readers could, however, extrapolate the points I make to their own situation.

My main purpose in writing this book, then, is to whet the appetite about what rational–emotive psychology has to offer in our understanding of how we as human beings restrict our psychological growth and how we might free ourselves from these restraints. If I succeed in this task and you wish to find out more about rational–emotive psychology and its applications, you will find some suggestions for further reading at the end of the book.

The development of REP

The roots of REP can be found in an approach to counselling and psychotherapy which can be placed in the cognitive–behavioural therapeutic tradition. This brief review of the development of REP will be structured around the three different names by which the therapeutic approach has been known: RT, RET and REBT.

Before 1955

The key year in the history of rational–emotive psychology is 1955; this date can be said to mark its birth. The originator of REP is an American clinical psychologist named Albert Ellis who became interested in psychotherapy after researching a book about a liberal approach to sex and sexuality. During his work for this volume, Ellis became known locally (in the Bronx borough of Manhattan) as an authority on sex and relationship problems. As such he was consulted by an increasing number of people who sought help for their own sex and love problems. Ellis found, somewhat to his surprise, that he enjoyed this work and was good at it; in fact he was able to help most of the people who sought his assistance.

Building on this development, Ellis founded the LAMP Institute

(LAMP stands for love and marital problems), but was advised by his lawyer to seek professional training if he wished to continue to practise in this field. As a result, because he saw his professional future in counselling and psychotherapy, Ellis decided to train as a clinical psychologist; this he did in the late 1940s.

Ellis's original orientation as a psychotherapist was psychoanalytical because he believed at the time that this was the deepest approach to therapy. However, he soon became disenchanted with his practice as a formal analyst, which involved seeing patients three or more times a week and the use of the couch. Although his patients were very appreciative of the work he was doing with them, and claimed that analysis was helping them, Ellis was dissatisfied with the results he was getting. He believed that, although his patients were feeling better, they were not getting better; for example, they seemed to be as fearful of disapproval and failure as they had been at the outset of analysis. Also, Ellis believed that the positive results that he was getting from analysis were very inefficient; it often took hundreds of sessions to bring about minimal gains.

This interest in the effectiveness and efficiency of therapeutic methods can be seen throughout Ellis's subsequent career in psychotherapy and provided the impetus for a period of investigation which led him to experiment with the seemingly less intense, face-to-face methods of psychodynamic psychotherapy and the modified analytic approach of Sandor Ferenczi, Ian Suttie and Izette de Forrest – they all recommended that therapists show their clients much more warmth than was customary in Freudian approaches to psychoanalysis and psychoanalytic psychotherapy.

Although the results he obtained from these modifications were an improvement, when compared with those he obtained from psychoanalysis, Ellis was still dissatisfied and continued his search for more effective and efficient therapeutic methods. This led him to experiment with an eclectic mix of analytic and non-analytic techniques. Once more his results improved, although again not to his satisfaction.

1955–1961

In the mid-1950s, Ellis decided to draw on his interests in applied philosophy and his past attempts to overcome his own personal problems in formulating a new approach to psychotherapy, an approach which he called rational therapy (RT). One of the core principles of RT was taken from Epictetus, a leading Stoic philosopher, who said 'Men are disturbed not by things but by their view of things'. In this respect, Ellis departed from the opinion of most of his contemporaries who, he felt, down-played the role that individuals' views play in their emotional problems. These views are basically ideas; Ellis held that when a person's ideas are irrational they lead to psychological problems, and when they are rational they lead to psychological health. Indeed, Ellis began to see that not only did psychoanalytic approaches neglect the ideational aspects of psychological disturbance, but that they also promoted what Ellis considered to be an irrational view, namely that a person's present problems are caused by unresolved conflicts in the past. I consider this issue in greater detail in Chapter 4. To distance himself from this irrational position and to stress the point that he was concerned about helping his clients to develop rational, and therefore, according to Ellis, more healthy ideas about themselves, other people and the world, he decided to call his new approach rational therapy.

In addition to this new emphasis on the ideas or views that his clients held–what psychologists today call cognition–Ellis held that to change troubling emotions and the irrational ideas that underpin them, a person needs to act against these ideas. He discovered this for himself when, earlier in his life, he resolved to overcome his shyness with women. Drawing upon the work of the early behaviourists, Ellis realised that the best way to tackle this problem was to push himself repeatedly to talk to women. He thus approached over 100 women in Bronx Botanical Gardens and spoke to each of them without any hesitation. Although a number walked away from Ellis immediately, most chose to chat with him. Interestingly, although Ellis asked many of these women for a date, only one agreed to meet him later–and she did not turn up for the date! It is thus surprising, given this lack of reinforcement, that Ellis claimed to have lost his shyness as a result of his endeavours. He was to say later of this episode that he realised that nothing terrible was going to happen to him. He just had a large number of pleasant conversations. Ellis thereby learned about the power of acting against one's fears, ensuring that behavioural assignments were to be a central part of his new therapy.

Far from giving an enthusiastic reception to Ellis's ideas, the psychotherapy world responded with hostility. In particular, he was criticised for advocating rationalism and for neglecting the realm of human emotion. Neither of these criticisms was valid, but both were given credence by the name Ellis gave to his approach–rational therapy. The first criticism–that Ellis was advocating rationalism (a school of thought which holds that humans can solve problems by pure reason alone)–was wrong; from the outset, Ellis has argued that although cognition is central to our understanding of how human beings disturb themselves and how they can overcome their problems, it is not the only factor that psychotherapists need to consider. For example, it is also important to understand emotions and the way people act in the world. Indeed, Ellis made this point in one of his first papers on RT (Ellis, 1958).

The second criticism – that RT neglected human emotion – was also untrue as has just been shown. However, as Ellis was keen to emphasise the distinctive aspects of his new approach – namely that therapists need to look for their clients' irrational ideas and help the clients to change these ideas – he did not perhaps stress enough the fact that he was neither advocating rationalism nor neglecting the emotions of his clients.

1961–1993

In 1961, keen to correct the erroneous impressions that others were forming of his therapeutic approach, Ellis decided to change the name to rational–emotive therapy (RET). By introducing the term 'emotive' into the title, Ellis was stressing not only that he was not neglecting his clients' emotions, but that therapy was an emotive experience for them rather than a dry, intellectual discussion as some critics wrongly claimed.

Now Ellis's critics changed tack. Instead of claiming that RET neglected emotions, they argued that it neglected behaviour. Once again this criticism fell far short of the mark because both RET and its predecessor RT argued that humans need to act against their irrational ideas if they are to change them and advocated the use of behavioural techniques as a central part of the therapeutic process.

1993 to the present

It was not until 1993, however, that Ellis decided to change the name of the therapy to rational emotive behaviour therapy (REBT). This somewhat unwieldy name shows quite clearly that the therapy, and the approach to psychology on which it is based, are concerned with cognition (in the form of rational and irrational ideas or beliefs), emotion and behaviour. It does not neglect any of these three interrelated psychological processes.

I mentioned earlier that rational–emotive psychology has been derived from the therapeutic approach currently known as REBT. I also noted that although Ellis (1978) has, somewhat reluctantly, sketched a rational–emotive framework for understanding personality, to date no-one has offered an integrated model that systematically applies rational emotive concepts to the broad area of psychology. Before starting my survey of those areas of psychology that have received attention from rational–emotive psychologists, let me consider the words 'rational' and 'emotive' (and related terms) as they are used in rational–emotive psychology.

Some important definitions
Rational and irrational

The terms 'rational' and 'irrational' are loaded words which people use in a very different way to that used in REP. Taking the term 'rational' first, in rational–emotive psychology, this word is used to describe people's healthy ideas or beliefs about themselves, other people and the world or life conditions. Rational beliefs have the following four main defining characteristics.

1. *They are flexible*: when people's beliefs are flexible, they can adjust readily to changing life circumstances, i.e. they can more easily 'roll with the punches' and deal more constructively with the 'slings and arrows of outrageous fortune' than they would if their beliefs were rigid.
2. *They are logical*: beliefs that are logical make sense and follow sensibly from, and fit well with, people's other rational beliefs.
3. *They are consistent with reality*: although certain theorists argue that there is no such thing as objective reality, rational–emotive psychologists hold that this view is too dogmatic, Thus, if a person holds a belief 'I am a fallible human being who fails at certain things and succeeds at others', this idea is deemed to be rational in that it is highly likely to be true. The person can prove both that she is a fallible human being and that she fails at certain tasks and succeeds at others.
4. *They help people to achieve their healthy goals and purposes*: people's beliefs have a pragmatic value. As such, they can consider their beliefs and their healthy goals and purposes, and thereby judge whether or not these beliefs help or hinder them in the pursuit of these goals. Rational beliefs promote goal achievement.

Conversely, irrational beliefs have the following four defining characteristics:

1. *They are rigid*: when people's beliefs are rigid or absolutistic, their responses to stressful situations are likely to be inflexible. Rather than accommodating such situations creatively, people try desperately to force reality to fit in with their pre–existing, fixed beliefs.
2. *They are illogical*: irrational beliefs often take the form of illogical conclusions from a person's rational beliefs. Thus, a person may rationally believe that it is desirable to receive approval from a significant 'other' and then illogically conclude that therefore such approval is absolutely necessary.
3. *They are inconsistent with reality*: for example, a person who

believes, 'I am a failure' is clearly holding a belief that is inconsistent with reality. Thus, if it were true that the person was a failure, he or she would have to fail at everything he or she does and literally never succeed at anything.
4. *They obstruct the person from achieving his healthy goals and purposes*: I mentioned earlier that people's beliefs have a pragmatic value. When they focus on the nature of their irrational beliefs and considers whether or not they help to achieve their valued goals, it frequently becomes clear that irrational beliefs hinder goal achievement (as shown in Chapter 3).

Emotion

The term 'emotion' (and its adjectival form 'emotive') has the same meaning in REP as it does in general. As REP has been derived from the therapeutic approach currently known as rational emotive behaviour therapy, it has much to say about emotions that are negative in feeling and less to say about positively tinged emotions. This is because, in common with therapists and counsellors from other therapeutic persuasions, REBT therapists deal much more frequently with their clients' negative emotions than with their positive emotions.

REP makes a unique contribution to the psychology of emotion by keenly discriminating between unhealthy negative emotions (such as anxiety, depresssion, guilt, shame, anger, hurt, morbid, suspicious jealousy and unhealthy envy) and healthy negative emotions (such as concern, sadness, remorse, regret, annoyance, disappointment, concern for one's relationship and healthy envy). REP also holds that it is important to be explicit about emotions and to avoid such vague feeling statements as 'I feel upset', 'I feel lousy' and 'I feel bad' because, in such statements, it is not clear whether the person is referring to a healthy or unhealthy negative emotion. In addition, REP maintains that it is important to be clear about the differences among negative emotions, particularly between healthy and unhealthy negative emotions, because making such clear distinctions enables identification of the beliefs underpinning the emotion under investigation. This issue is discussed more fully in Chapter 5.

The ABC framework

At the core of rational–emotive psychology is a framework for understanding psychological problems and well-being. Although at first sight this framework will appear simple, even overly simplistic, it can help us to understand a complex set of psychological phenomena, as shown in Chapter 8. However, here the simple version of the ABC framework is presented as a schematic form in Figure 1.1.

A: Activating events (including interpretations and inferences of the event)

B: Beliefs

C: Consequences (emotional and behavioural consequences of holding the beliefs at B)

Figure 1.1: Simple ABC Framework

In the next three chapters I discuss carefully each element of this framework, starting with the A's (activating events).

Chapter 2
Activating events

An activating event (A) is a situation, or an aspect of a situation, which can potentially serve to trigger a person's belief. A's can be actual situations or they can be interpreted or inferred, and the role of interpretations and inferences are discussed later in this chapter. I also discuss other important facets of activating events.

A's can be broad or specific

An activating event can be either a global situation or a specific aspect of this global situation. For example, I am writing this chapter in a coffee bar at Waterloo station. This situation can be a broad A. When I stop writing, however, and scan my environment, my attention is caught by a small white bear, wearing a Santa Claus hat, that is nestling in a red sock and hanging above the serving area. As I am smiling with faint pleasure, I realise that this bear is currenly serving as a specific A and is triggering a positive belief at B. Note that the bear is only one small part of the broader context in which I find myself and it is only one of a large number of specific A's on which I could potentially focus. I could focus more broadly on the larger context in which I am sitting, however, and that could trigger a belief and therefore serve as an A.

A's can be past, present or future events

Given that an A is an activating event, it can refer to an event that is currently occurring. Thus, as I write this sentence, the tube train in which I am sitting has just left Baker Street station. Note that this statement constitutes a broad A and theoretically I could focus on only one of a number of presently-occurring, specific activating events that constitute my current total environment.

Now if I wanted to I could think of an event that I experienced in the past. As I do so, I focus on the Arsenal cap that I bought last

Monday afternoon when the team played Queens Park Rangers at home. The fact that I recall this event with some pleasure means that this purchase constitutes a specific, past A that triggers a belief. If I broaden my attention and think of the match itself, which finished as an unsatisfactory 0–0 draw, my mood changes to disappointment. Thus, the match itself constitutes a broader past A which is triggering a different belief.

As mentioned above, A's can also refer to future events. Thus, in a month's time I am going to a colleague's book launch. Although, of course, I do not know what the evening will be like, I can construct a likely scenario in my mind. I can focus on the general picture that I have of the evening and as I do so the evening constitutes a broad, future A. I can also focus in my mind's eye on possible specific events that may happen that evening, such as the display of my colleague's books or the brief talk that she is likely to give about the book. As such, these events constitute specific, future A's.

A's can refer to external or internal events

So far, I have considered events that have occurred, are occurring or are likely to occur out there in the world. As such they can be viewed as external A's. However, A's can also refer to events that occur within us: internal A's. Examples of internal A's include twinges or pains that we experience in our bodies; other bodily sensations that we may interpret or infer as hunger or thirst; thoughts; intentions to act in certain ways; and images, dreams, nightmares, daydreams and fantasies.

Indeed, even our emotions can serve as internal A's, although emotions are frequently interpretations or inferences that we make from our bodily states and the context in which we find ourselves (see below for a full discussion of interpretations and inferences). In any case, when we focus on the way we feel, these emotions can trigger beliefs that lead us to further feelings. Thus, as I discuss more fully in Chapter 7, we can feel anxious about our anxiety, guilty about our angry feelings, and can be ashamed of being envious, amongst others.

A's can be actual, interpreted or inferred

Understanding activating events can be quite a complex process. To complicate matters even more, A's can refer to actual events, events that are interpreted by the person and those where the person makes inferences that are personally significant. I begin the discussion by looking at actual A's before considering and distinguishing between interpretations and inferences.

Distinguishing between actual A's and interpretations

Imagine the following. We are sitting down having a discussion and I suddenly get up, walk over to the window and put my face to the window pane. I then ask you to describe exactly what I am doing. In response, you might say that I was looking out of the window. If you did say this, you would not be describing exactly what I was doing. You would be making an interpretation of what I was doing, since you cannot know from the information available to you whether or not I have my eyes open. To make an actual description of what I was doing you would have to say something like: 'You are standing with your face near to the window.' So a description, or an actual A, does not add to what can be actually observed (in this case), while an interpretation goes beyond the data at hand. An interpretation, therefore, can be regarded as a hypothesis about a reality that needs to be tested. Of course an interpretation can be correct. I could well have had my eyes open and have been looking out of the window; but the point is that you could have been wrong. Therefore, it is important to distinguish between a description and an interpretation when thinking about activating events. Incidentally, you can of course make errors in description. Thus, if in the window example you said that I was standing facing a painting of a window you would be incorrect in your attempt to describe what I was doing. If you said that I was looking out of the painting of a window, you would be incorrect at both the levels of description and interpretation.

Distinguishing between interpretations and inferences

In the above example, I mentioned that an interpretation goes beyond the data at hand. So do inferences, however, and so what are the differences between interpretations and inferences? I regard a statement that goes beyond the data at hand as an interpretation when it is not personally significant. Whereas an inference is a statement that goes beyond the data at hand and is of personal significance. When a statement is of personal significance, the person making the inference experiences an emotion, which they would not experience with a non-personally significant interpretation. An inference does not directly lead to emotional experience, but rather is associated with it.

Let me return to the window example to clarify the difference between an interpretation and an inference. The statement that I discussed in that example, 'You are looking out of the window', is an interpretation by my definition, because it both goes beyond the data at hand, and, in all probability, it does not have personal significance for the person making the statement. Therefore, it is not accompanied by an emotional experience of any note.

However, let us assume that in answer to my request for you to describe what I was doing, you replied, 'You are trying to make a fool out of me', a statement which was accompanied by a feeling of irritation. This would be an inference because it both goes beyond the data at hand, and, in all probability, it does have personal significance for you. The evidence for 'personal significance' in your statement is that it involves a presumed judgment of you by another (that I am taking you for a fool) and it is accompanied by an emotion. If your statement was not accompanied by any emotion, it could more properly be viewed as an interpretation. So, inferences tend to be accompanied by emotion whereas interpretations are made without the accompaniment of emotion.

Inferences and the personal domain

In the mid 1970s, Aaron T. Beck (1976), a noted American psychiatrist published a book entitled *'Cognitive Therapy and the Emotional Disorders'*. This was the first book to outline the principles of cognitive therapy, an approach which is currently in vogue in the psychotherapy world on both sides of the Atlantic. In this book, Beck wrote about a concept which he called the 'personal domain', a kind of psychological space which contains issues of personal significance. Examples of such issues might include: the way you are viewed by others, the well-being of your children, respect for your country's flag, and the boundary between your property and that of your neighbours. Your personal domain includes both issues that concern you directly as a person and issues that do not so concern you, but have personal significance for you.

Let me give you an example of the latter. I once attended a workshop on anger run by one of the world's leading authorities on the subject. During the workshop he was asked what he would get very angry about. He replied that seeing someone burn the American flag in front of him would provoke an angry, even aggressive response in him. Note that this event would not be directed at him personally, but would be directed at something which occupied a central place of significance in his personal domain, i.e. his respect for the American flag and all that this symbol stood for in his mind.

This example sheds light on another issue concerning inferences and emotions. Remember first that I am not saying that inferences lead directly to emotional experiences: they do not, as I discuss in Chapter 4. However, they are correlated with emotions; inferences and emotions tend to go together. What the 'burning of the American flag' example shows is that strong emotions are associated with inferences of great personal significance, i.e. that occupy an important place in the personal domain. Conversely, the less personally significant the inference, the less intense will be that person's emotional response. Thus, the man's emotional response to the burning of a flag of any other nation will probably be less intense, because the inference 'disrespect is being shown to this country's flag' is less personally significant to him than would be his inference 'disrespect is being shown to the American flag'.

In his book, Beck noted that different kinds of inferences with respect to one's personal domain are related to different emotions and I discuss this fully in Chapters 5 and 7.

A's that trigger beliefs are crucial in understanding the emotional and behavioural consequences of holding these beliefs

So far I have distinguished between actual, interpreted and inferred A's. In order to understand a person's emotions and behaviour, it is important to understand that person's beliefs in the context of his or her feelings and actions. However, beliefs do not exist in a vacuum; some kind of activating event needs to be present in order for a person's belief to be triggered. I call such an event a critical activating event (Beal, personal communication).

I have stated that inferences are personally significant statements that go beyond the data at hand. As such, inferences frequently serve as critical activating events, because they often co-exist with a person's emotional experience. Interpretations rarely serve as critical A's, because, by definition, they do not have significance for the individual.

Actual activating events can also serve as critical A's when they are personally significant accurate descriptions of reality (e.g. the death of a loved one).

Given that human beings frequently respond to the views they take of events rather than the events themselves and because inferences are a core feature of these views, we will find more often that inferences rather than actual A's will serve as critical A's .

The chaining of actual A's, interpretations and inferences and the triggering of beliefs

I have made the point that in a given situation, there are many actual A's that can potentially trigger the beliefs of the person in that situation. The same is true when we consider the inferences that a person might make of a situation. When that person experiences an emotion about the situation (e.g. anxiety), it is important to discover which of the inferences he or she is making is critical (i.e. has triggered her anxiety-related belief) in order to understand fully what he or she is anxious about.

Let me give an example of this. In an episode of the television series 'Mash', two of the central characters, B.J. and Hawkeye were in their tent late at night. Hawkeye is trying to sleep, but cannot do so because B.J. is tossing and turning restlessly. Eventually, Hawkeye persuades B.J. to discuss what is on his mind so that they can both get some sleep. The following is roughly what was said between them.

Hawkeye: So what are you so het up about?

B.J.: I received a letter from Peg [his wife] and she tells me that it is raining at home.

[The letter is a broad actual A and the part about it raining at home is a specific actual A on which B.J. has focussed.]

Hawkeye: So it's raining at home. What's there to be worried about?

B.J.: Well, the guttering is broken and Peg will try to fix it herself.

[The statement 'the guttering is broken' is an actual A, whereas 'Peg will try to fix it herself' is an interpretation.]

Hawkeye: So?

B.J.: Well, the ladder is broken.

[This statement is an actual A]

Hawkeye: Oh, I know what you're worried about. You're scared that she won't see that the ladder is broken and will fall and injure herself. Well, Peg is bound to see that it is broken, won't attempt to climb it and will therefore be safe. So there is nothing to worry about. Now let's get some sleep.

In his impatience to get some sleep, Hawkeye makes a number of interpretations: one that he assumes B.J. is making, 'Peg won't see that the ladder is broken' and two that he makes himself, 'Peg is bound to see that it is broken' and she 'won't attempt to climb it'. These are interpretations because as they are stated, they do not have any personal significance for himself or for B.J. Thus, the statement – Peg won't attempt to climb a broken ladder – on its own does not have any personal significance for himself or B.J., if B.J. were to make it. Rather, it is the inference – she will be safe – that provides such significance. As Hawkeye is a very good friend of B.J. and cares about what happens to B.J.'s wife, the statement – Peg will be safe – is an inference for him. If he did not care about what happened to Peg, this statement would be an interpretation. If B.J. were to make it, it would, of course, be an inference.

Hawkeye also makes a number of inferences. First, he makes an inference that he assumes B.J. is making (that Peg 'will fall and injure herself'). Again this is an inference because Hawkeye cares about what happens to Peg. If B.J. were to say such a thing it would obviously be an inference. Second, Hawkeye makes an inference of his own (that 'Peg will be safe') – as already discussed above.

Hawkeye's response typifies the fact that we often assume that we know what another person is worried about based on what that person has just said. Like Hawkeye, as we shall see, we are often wrong.

B.J.: No, you don't understand. I am sure that she will see that the ladder is broken [interpretation] and she will ask the local odd job man to fix it [interpretation].

Hawkeye: So what are you worried about?

B.J.: Well, she'll soon discover that the odd job man has retired [actual A] and she'll ask our next door neighbour for help instead [interpretation].

Hawkeye: And?

B.J.: Well, the next door neighbour may make a pass at her.

[Whether or not his wife responds to the next door neighbour's advance, this is probably an inference because B.J., as portrayed in the series, is the kind of man to be concerned about this. If he did not care, it would be an interpretation].

Hawkeye: But, you can trust Peg. She's not the kind of woman to have sex with another man.

[Since Hawkeye, in this episode, is pleased about this, it has personal significance for him and is therefore an inference.]

B.J: But, I've been over here for two years and therefore she has been without sex for two years [actual A]. So I'm really scared that she will sleep with him. I couldn't stand it if she did.

[The statement – 'she will sleep with him' – is obviously an inference.]

This example clearly shows that actual A's, interpretations and inferences are linked together in a kind of chain and that frequently one has to pursue this chain to find the actual A or, more frequently, the inference that triggers the person's belief. In the 'Mash' example, B.J.'s statement that his wife might sleep with his next door neighbour constituted a critical A because it was this he was most worried about.

It is important to note that a critical A can occur anywhere in a chain. The important points to remember are: (1) a critical A is the A in a chain that is most closely linked to the person's emotion; and (2) when discovered, a critical A often leads the person to express his or her belief spontaneously in words. Put another way, this A often triggers awareness and verbalisation of the belief.

In the above example, B.J.'s inference – 'she will sleep with him' – triggered the belief – 'I couldn't stand it if she did'.

Having discussed some of the important facets of activating events, I shall now consider the heart of rational-emotive psychology, namely the role that beliefs play in psychological health and disturbance.

Chapter 3
Beliefs

In this chapter, I consider the role that beliefs play in psychological problems and psychological health. As I have already mentioned in previous chapters, beliefs occupy a central place in rational-emotive psychology. But what are beliefs according to REP?

The nature of beliefs

In Chapter 2, I carefully considered the nature of activating events (A's). In particular, I distinguished between actual A's, which reflect the observable reality of a situation, and the interpretations and inferences which, although possibly correct, go beyond the data at hand. As such, interpretations and inferences can both be regarded as cognitions in that they both reflect the thoughts that people have about situations.

You will recall from Figure 1.1. (see p.8), which showed the simplified ABC model, that A stands for an activating event and B stands for a person's belief about that event. Clearly a person's belief is a cognition in that it reflects his or her attitude to the A. What I am also saying, however, is that interpretations and inferences are also cognitions which add to the observable nature of the event. What they add, however, is very different to what is added when a person brings his or her belief into the picture. Thus, an A involves both an actual event and a person's thoughts about that event, while B involves a different type of thought about the A.

It is this difference between interpretations and inferences on the one hand, and beliefs on the other, that represents one of REP's unique contributions to understanding human emotion and behaviour. What is the nature of this difference?

Beliefs are evaluative

An evaluation involves a person making a judgment about something.

It involves making a rating or assigning a value to that which is being evaluated. According to REP, a person's beliefs are clearly evaluative. Furthermore, REP states that it is possible to be quite precise about the nature of a person's beliefs. This is particularly important when distinguishing between rational beliefs and irrational beliefs.

Interpretations are clearly different from beliefs. As I define them, interpretations go beyond the data at hand and do not involve issues that are significant to the person. As such, they are clearly non-evaluative, whereas evaluation is the defining characteristic of a person's beliefs.

Distinguishing between inferences and beliefs is more difficult, but still possible. Inferences, if you recall, go beyond the data at hand and involve issues that are significant to the person. As they involve issues that are significant to the person and as the concept of personal significance has, by its very nature, an evaluative component, thus inferences themselves have an evaluative component. This evaluative component, however, is not precisely stated in inferences as it is in beliefs. Let me illustrate this.

In the previous chapter, I outlined a dialogue between two characters from the television series, 'Mash' – Hawkeye and B.J. – to demonstrate the fact that actual A's, interpretations and inferences are often linked together in a chain. You will recall that the aspect of the overall A that triggered B.J.'s belief (i.e. the critical A) was the inference: 'my wife will sleep with the next door neighbour'. This inference triggered in B.J. the belief: 'I couldn't stand it if that happened'. This statement is a belief because it is clearly evaluative. Yet, B.J. could have had a number of other beliefs concerning the possibility of his wife sleeping with the next door neighbour. For example, he could have had the belief: 'I wouldn't like it if that happened, but it wouldn't be the end of the world', or even 'It would be good if that happened. I know that my wife likes sex and I don't like to think of her going without it for so long'. The point is that by itself an inference does not indicate the full extent of the way in which a person evaluates a situation. Rather, if the inference is central enough in a particular situation, it triggers the person's belief. In this case the inference is known as a critical A.

In summary, an interpretion goes beyond the data at hand and is usually about something that does not have significance for the person. As such, an interpretation is non-evaluative. An inference also goes beyond the data at hand, but is usually about something that has significance for the person. As such it has an evaluative element. However, given that a person can have different beliefs about the same inference, the latter contains insufficient information to constitute a belief. On the other hand, beliefs contain precise evaluative information and are fully evaluative.

Beliefs can be rational or irrational

In Chapter 1, I defined the terms 'rational' and 'irrational' as they are used in REP with respect to a person's beliefs (see pp. 6–7). I have summarised these points in Figure 3.1.

RATIONAL BELIEFS	IRRATIONAL BELIEFS
Flexible	Rigid/Absolutistic
Logical	Illogical
Consistent with Reality	Inconsistent with Reality
Promotes Goal Achievement	Hinders Goal Achievement

Figure 3.1. Characteristics of Rational and Irrational Beliefs

Types of rational and irrational beliefs

According to REP, there are four main types of rational and irrational beliefs (see Figure 3.2). I consider one rational-irrational pairing at a time and begin my discussion by writing about the rational belief.

RATIONAL BELIEFS	IRRATIONAL BELIEFS
Preferential/Desiring	Musturbatory
Anti-Awfulising	Awfulising
High Frustration Tolerance	Low Frustration Tolerance
Acceptance	Condemning/Downing

Figure 3.2. Types of Rational and Irrational Beliefs

Preferential/desiring beliefs vs musturbatory beliefs

I have stressed in this chapter that beliefs are evaluative; that is they represent a value stance towards the object being evaluated. The main ways in which this can be expressed concern a person's preferences and desires, on the one hand, and what he thinks he must get, on the other. Let me consider preferential/desiring beliefs first.

If I prefer to get a job promotion, I am indicating that I place a relative positive value on this promotion and would rather achieve it. Conversely, when I say that I would prefer not to be laughed at by my peer group, I am indicating that I place a relative negative value on this ridicule and would rather not receive it. Preferential/desiring beliefs also take the form: 'I wish', 'I want', 'I would like', 'it would be nice if...' among others.

Given that one of the defining characteristics of a rational belief is flexibility, it is important to make clear that a preference is non-dogmatic. The way that this is done is to spell out what Brian Kelly, an Irish rational-emotive psychologist, calls a full preference statement. Putting the two rational beliefs that I introduced in the previous paragraph into the form of full preference statements, we have:

1. I prefer to get a job promotion, *but I do not have to achieve it.*
2. I would prefer not to be laughed at by my peer group, *but there is no reason why they must not laugh at me.*

You will note from these two sentences that there are two parts to each belief. The first part asserts the preference, while the second, in italics, negates the possibility of rigidity. If the second part of the belief were not made explicit, it would be possible for the person to change implicitly the rational, preference belief into an irrational, 'musturbatory' belief; thus:

1. I prefer to get a job promotion (and therefore I have to achieve it).
2. I would prefer not to be laughed at by my peer group (and therefore they must not laugh at me).

I mentioned above that if the full preference form of a rational belief is not made explicit, then there is a danger that the person will implicitly change his or her rational belief into a musturbatory, irrational belief. I have stressed the word implicitly here because this process often occurs below the person's awareness and therefore the implicit musturbatory belief does not feature in the person's verbalisation.

You will recall that one of the defining characteristics of a rational belief is that it is flexible. Preferential/desiring beliefs are flexible because, by their very nature, they allow for the fact that a person may not get what he or she wants, or may get what he or she does *not* want.

Preferential/desiring beliefs also meet three other criteria for rationality. First, they are logical. A person's specific preferences make sense in that they point to what the person values and they are also logically related to the broader concept of his or her general desires. Thus, if I prefer to get what I desire (general belief), then it is perfectly logical for me to say that I prefer to get a desired promotion (specific belief). My specific preference logically follows from the broader proposition that I prefer to get what I want.

Second, preferential/desiring beliefs are consistent with reality. In this case, it is consistent with the reality of my innermost desires for me to say that I would like to get promoted—assuming, of course, that I am not lying and this is really what I believe.

Third, preferential/desiring beliefs promote goal achievement. If I wish to get promoted, but do not insist that I must be successful, then I am motivated to do well. I am more able, therfore, to channel my motivation into productive action than I would be if I believed that I must get promoted, in which case I would be desperate and this desperation would impede my ability to work well and plan constructively. Also, if I did not care whether or not I got promoted, I would not be motivated to work towards this end and would significantly reduce my chances of getting it.

Now let me consider musturbatory beliefs. You will recall that I have discussed two examples of rational beliefs (see p.20):

1. I prefer to get a job promotion, but I do not have to achieve it.
2. I would prefer not to be be laughed at by my peer group, but there is no reason why they must not laugh at me.

Now let me present the irrational form of these beliefs:

1. I have to get a job promotion.
2. I must not be laughed at by my peer group.

If I believe that I must get a job promotion, I am indicating that I place an absolute positive value on this accomplishment and that it is absolutely necessary that I achieve it. Conversely, when I say that I must not be laughed at by my peer group, I am indicating that I place an absolute negative value on this ridicule and that it is absolutely necessary that I avoid it.

Musturbatory beliefs also take the form: 'I absolutely should', 'I've got to', 'I ought to', 'I demand', 'it is absolutely necessary that...' among others.

Given that one of the defining characteristics of an irrational belief is rigidity and absolutism, it is important to make clear that musturbatory beliefs are dogmatic. They do not allow for the fact that a person may not get what he wants or may get what he does not want.

Musturbatory beliefs also meet the other three criteria for irrationality. First, they are illogical in the sense that they do not logically follow from the person's preferences. Thus if I prefer to get a job promotion, it is illogical for me to say that I must be promoted. The two beliefs are not connected in any logical fashion.

Second, musturbatory beliefs are inconsistent with reality. If there was a law of the universe that decreed that I must get my job promotion then I would have to get it, no matter how I behaved at work. Since there is no such law, we can conlude that this demand is inconsistent with reality.

Third, musturbatory beliefs hinder goal achievement. As I said earlier (see p.21), if I believe that I must get promoted then I would be desperate or anxious and these states would impede my ability to work productively and plan constructively, thus lessening my chances of getting the promotion.

The primacy of musts and preferences

As Figure 3.2 shows there are three other sets of rational and irrational beliefs that need to be considered: anti-awfulising versus awfulising; high frustration tolerance versus low frustration tolerance, and acceptance versus condemnation/downing. Before I do this, I want to discuss one important issue. Taken together, the four rational beliefs constitute a rational philosophy whereas the four irrational beliefs constitute an irrational philosophy. However, rational-emotive psychologists are divided in their consideration of the centrality of specific rational and irrational beliefs in accounting for psychological disturbance and health. Let me deal with this issue by considering irrational beliefs.

Some rational-emotive psychologists, including Albert Ellis, hold that musturbatory beliefs are primary in a person's thinking and that the other three types of irrational beliefs are derived from these musts. In particular, Ellis (1983) argues that the essence of psychological disturbance is rigidity, dogmatism, absolutism or religiosity. Thus, Ellis and his supporters on this issue argue that when I hold the belief: 'I must get a job promotion and it is awful if I don't', the must has primacy in my thinking and my awfulising belief is derived from this must. Thus, they would argue also that the reason why I think that it is awful if I do not get my job promotion is because I believe that I must achieve it.

Other rational-emotive psychologists hold the opposing view. Their opinion is that my awfulising belief (in this case, although the same argument would hold with low frustration tolerance and condemnation/downing beliefs) has primacy in my thinking and that my musturbatory belief is derived from my awfulising belief. They would argue that the reason why I think that I must get promoted at work is because I believe that it would be awful if I did not achieve the promotion.

Yet, other rational-emotive psychologists consider that musturbatory beliefs and the three other types of irrational beliefs are opposite sides of the same cognitive coin, and thus, because they go together, no one type of irrational belief has primacy.

As yet we have no research evidence to settle this issue. What this debate does show, however, is that the field of REP is a dynamic one and that rational-emotive psychologists have independent minds and do not unthinkingly agree with the views of Albert Ellis.

Anti-awfulising beliefs versus awfulising beliefs

The second set of evaluative beliefs that I consider now relate to a person's appraisal of how good or bad it is that given circumstances exist or do not exist. This appraisal may relate to past, present or future circumstances. Let me consider anti-awfulising beliefs first. In doing so, I take the position favoured by Albert Ellis and some other rational-emotive psychologists that such beliefs are derivatives of preferential/desiring beliefs.

If I prefer to get a job promotion, but do not demand that I must achieve it, then I will tend to conclude that it would be bad if I fail to get promoted. This conclusion indicates that I place a relative negative value on my failure.

As I noted earlier in this chapter, it is often important to give the full version of a rational belief. In the case of an anti-awfulising belief, this would be: 'It would be bad if I failed to be promoted, but not terrible'. As this example shows, there are two parts to an anti-awfulising belief. The first part provides an evaluation of badness, while the second part negates the possibility of awfulising. One point needs particular emphasis. What makes an anti-awfulising belief rational is the fact that it is not extreme. Through it the person recognises that, even though it may be very, very bad that a tragic set of circumstances exists, things could be worse. Thus, the belief, 'It is very, very bad that this set of circumstances exists', is rational even though it contains a very strong negative evaluation. A rational belief, therefore, can contain such a very strong negative evaluation as long as it is not extreme. Extremity is a defining characteristic of an awfulising belief, not of an anti-awfulising one. The latter is a rating of how bad it is that an activating event exists which can be flexibly placed on a continuum of badness ranging from 1–99.99 per cent.

Anti-awfulising beliefs also meet the other three criteria for rationality. First, they are logical. A person's specific anti-awfulising beliefs make sense in that they point to what the person values and also they are logically related to the broader concept of his general anti-awfulising philosophy. Thus, if I believe that it is bad when I do not get what I want (general belief), then it is perfectly logical for me to say that it would be bad if I did not get a desired job promotion (specific belief).

Second, anti-awfulising beliefs are consistent with reality. In this case, it is consistent with the reality of my inner evaluation for me to say that it would be bad if I were not to achieve a job promotion –

assuming once again that I am not lying and this is really what I believe. Also, I can prove that it is bad not to be promoted in that I can point to some of the disadvantages that will result if I fail to be promoted.

Third, anti-awfulising beliefs promote goal achievement. If I consider it to be bad that I may not get my job promotion, but not terrible, this belief will motivate me to do well and will help me more effectively to translate my motivation into constructive action than would the corresponding awfulising belief. Also, if I believe that it is neither good nor bad to get promoted, I would be apathetic and would not strive towards achieving the promotion. This would limit my chances of actually obtaining it.

One last point on anti-awfulising beliefs. As I am taking the position here that anti-awfulising beliefs are derivatives of preferential/desiring beliefs, it follows that when I have a strong preference for an event to occur (e.g. my job promotion) and it does not happen, then my anti-awfulising belief will be more strongly negative than it would be if my preference was moderate or mild.

Now let me consider awfulising beliefs. If I believe that I must get a job promotion, then I will tend to conclude that it would be awful if I did not achieve it. According to Ellis, awfulising means both worse than 100 per cent bad and worse that it absolutely should or must be. Note how my awfulising belief is derived from my musturbatory thinking.

Awfulising beliefs can also take the form: 'It is terrible that...', 'It is horrible that...' and 'It is the end of the world that ...'. I want to make it clear that when the words 'awful', 'horrible' and 'terrible' are employed in describing irrational beliefs, they are used in a grossly exaggerated manner. I stress this point because the same words can have a different meaning. For example, when I say 'It is terrible that it is raining', I really mean that it is burdensome that it is raining. I am not using it to imply that it is the end of the world. As such, I would not be thinking irrationally and therefore would not be emotionally disturbed. Here and elsewhere REP stresses that it is important to distinguish between a word and its meaning (Dryden, 1986).

Awfulising beliefs meet the four criteria for irrationality. Given that these beliefs are grossly exaggerated appraisals that are to be found at the very extreme end of the evaluative scale, they meet the criterion of absolutism. Thus, when I say that it is awful should I fail to get my job promotion, at that moment (or for however long my awfulising belief is activated), I tend to believe that nothing could be worse.

Second, awfulising beliefs are illogical in the sense that they do not follow logically from a person's realistic evaluations of a situation. If I believe, rationally, that it would be bad, but not terrible for me not to be promoted, it is illogical for me to jump to the conclusion that it would be terrible to miss out on the promotion. My anti-awfulising and awfulising beliefs are not connected in any logical manner.

Third, awfulising beliefs are inconsistent with reality. If it were true that it is terrible that I may not get promoted, then nothing could be worse. As, I can think of many things worse than not getting promoted, we can conclude that my awfulising belief is not consistent with reality.

Finally, awfulising beliefs hinder goal achievement. As I said earlier (see p. 25) if I believe that it would be terrible if I were to fail to achieve promotion, then I would be desperate or anxious and these emotional states would interfere with my ability to work productively and plan constructively, thereby decreasing my chances of achieving promotion. Also, if I actually failed to achieve promotion, my awfulising belief would inhibit me from adjusting to this activating event and interfere with my clarity of thought concerning how I might rectify the situation.

High frustration tolerance beliefs versus low frustration tolerance beliefs

The third set of evaluative beliefs relate to a person's appraisal of how well or poorly he or she can tolerate a particular event. As with anti-awfulising and awfulising beliefs, this appraisal may relate to the past, present or future. I consider high frustration tolerance (HFT) beliefs first and again take the position that such beliefs are derivatives of preferential/desiring beliefs.

If I prefer to get a job promotion, but do not demand that I must obtain it, then I will conclude that I could stand it if I fail to get promoted. The full version of this high frustration belief would be: 'It would be difficult to tolerate not getting my promotion, but I could withstand it'. Note that there are two parts to this high frustration tolerance belief. The first part acknowledges that not getting what I desire would be difficult to tolerate, while the second part negates the possibility of my falling apart (low frustration tolerance belief). Also, the part of the belief that states that it would be difficult to tolerate not getting what I want prevents me from jumping to a belief of indifference, for example 'As I could withstand not getting my job promotion, it would not matter if I did not obtain it'. As with anti-awfulising beliefs, HFT beliefs are rational because they are not extreme. The belief 'I would find it very, very difficult to tolerate this tragic event if it happened, but I still could withstand it' is rational because, although it contains a very strong negative evaluation, it is not extreme. I am still tolerating a very negative situation. So, extremity is a defining characteristic of a low frustration tolerance (LFT) belief, not of an HFT one. The latter means that I will not die if a negative set of circumstances exists or that I can foresee the prospect of happiness in the future even if these circumstances continue.

HFT beliefs also meet the other criteria for rationality. First, they are logical. A person's specific HFT beliefs make sense because they point to what he or she values and they are also logically related to his or her broader HFT philosophy. Thus, if I believe that I can withstand negative events in general, even though I find it difficult to tolerate them, then it is logical for me to say that, while I would find it difficult to tolerate, I could withstand a specific event such as not obtaining a job promotion.

Second, HFT beliefs are consistent with reality. In this case, it is realistic for me to say that I can withstand not being promoted, even though it would be difficult to tolerate. Indeed, empirically I am able to prove that I can withstand such an event even when I tell myself irrationally that I cannot do so. Even when I have such an LFT belief, I am withstanding the situation because I have neither died nor have I foresaken the possibility of future happiness.

Third, HFT beliefs aid goal achievement. If I show myself that I can withstand not getting promoted, even though it would be difficult, this belief will be more likely to help me both to concentrate in advance on what I need to do to further my chances of winning promotion, and to persist after the fact at continuing to strive for my goal should I be unsuccessful on this given occasion, than would the corresponding LFT belief, i.e 'I can not withstand the prospect of not getting promoted'.

Finally, since HFT beliefs are derivatives of preferential/desiring beliefs, the stronger my preference, the harder it will be for me to tolerate it if my preference is not met. However, even if my strongest desire is unfulfilled, holding an HFT belief means that I will be able to tolerate this state of affairs (although of course it will severely tax my resources).

Let me consider low frustration tolerance (LFT) beliefs. If I believe that I must get a job promotion, then I will tend to conclude that I could not stand it if I did not achieve it. According to Ellis, holding an LFT belief consists of two meanings. First, it means that I believe I would disintegrate or die if the activating event that went counter to my 'must' happened at A. Second, it means that if this activating event occurred, I believe that I will never again experience any happiness as long as it exists, or worse because it has happened. Note how my LFT belief is derived from my musturbatory belief.

LFT beliefs can take a variety of forms, e.g. 'I can't stand it...', 'It is unbearable...', 'I would die...', 'I would fall apart...', among others. As the term LFT makes clear, these terms point to a person's perceived ability to tolerate frustation or discomfort. Again, it is important to distinguish between words and their meaning. We often use phrases such as 'I can't stand it' in a casual fashion when we really mean 'I don't like it' or 'I strongly dislike it'. When this is the case we would not be thinking irrationally and therefore would not be emotionally disturbed although we would experience negative feelings. When we use the term, 'I can't stand it' in the way that Ellis defines it, however, then we are thinking irrationally and are emotionally disturbed.

LFT beliefs meet the four criteria for irrationality. Given that the person is saying that he cannot stand a situation, this represents an extreme statement and as such this belief meets the criterion of absolutism. Thus, when I say that I could not stand it should I fail to get my job promotion at that moment (or for however long my LFT belief is activated), I believe both that I would disintegrate if I were to fail to be promoted and that I could never be happy again if this were to transpire. These two statements are extreme and therefore absolutistic.

Second, LFT beliefs are illogical in the sense that they do not follow logically from a person's realistic struggle to tolerate negative activating events. If I believe, rationally, that not getting my promotion would be difficult to bear, it is illogical for me to jump to the conclusion that it would be unbearable. My HFT and LFT beliefs are not connected in any logical fashion.

Third, LFT beliefs are inconsistent with reality. If it were true that I could not stand not getting promoted, the I would literally disintegrate or would never experience happiness again, both of these beliefs are highly unlikely outcomes. Even when I am telling myself that I can not withstand not getting promoted, I am withstanding it. I may be emotionally disturbed, but I have not disintegrated or forfeited the possibility for future happiness. Consequently, my LFT belief is not consistent with reality.

Finally, LFT beliefs hinder goal achievement. If I believe that I could not withstand it if I failed to achieve promotion, then this belief would lead me to be anxious about the prospect about not achieving it, a feeling which would again interfere with my ability to work productively and plan constructively, thereby decreasing my chances of achieving promotion. Furthermore, if I actually failed to get promotion, my LFT belief would interfere with my ability to adjust to this activating event and with my thoughts about how I might rectify the situation.

Acceptance beliefs versus condemning/downing beliefs

The final set of evaluative beliefs concern a person's attitude towards self, others and life conditions. I consider the rational belief – in this case acceptance – first. Again, I assume that acceptance beliefs are derived from preferential/desiring beliefs.

If I prefer to get a job promotion, but do not demand that I must be awarded it, then I will tend to make the following appraisals. First, I will tend to accept myself as a fallible human being who is a complex mixture of positive, negative and neutral aspects. Then, if I do not achieve promotion, I will reflect on this situation and if I discover that my lack of success on this occasion can be attributed to any deficiencies in my performance at work, I will rate these negatively, but will accept myself as a fallible human being who has not performed as well as I would have liked.

Second, I will accept other people who are involved as fallible human beings who are a complex mixture of positive, negative and neutral aspects. Thus, if I fail to get promoted and learn that this was due to an unfavourable job appraisal from my supervisor that I consider to be unfair, I will dislike his unjust appraisal, but will accept him as a fallible human being who has acted, in my opinion, in an unfair manner.

Third, I will accept the situation that I am in without putting it down. Thus, if I fail to obtain my promotion, I will dislike this fact, but will still view the company that I work for as a complex mixture of good, bad and neutral elements.

Using the full form of these acceptance beliefs, I will express them as follows:

1. I did not receive a job promotion which was mainly, I see now, due to my deficiencies at work. I can accept myself as a fallible human being for my deficiencies even though I regret them. I am not less worthy for having them.
   [In this belief I have asserted the fact that I am a fallible human being, evaluated my deficiencies negatively and denied that I am less worthy for having them.]
2. I did not receive a job promotion which was mainly, I see now, due to my supervisor giving me a negative appraisal which I consider unfair. I can accept him as a fallible human being, but I really dislike his behaviour. However, he is not less worthy for acting as he did.
   [In this belief I have asserted the fact that my supervisor is a fallible human being, evaluated his behaviour negatively and denied that he is less worthy for his action.]
3. Even though the company denied me a promotion which I do not like, it is a complex organisation with good, bad and neutral parts. It is not a lousy company for depriving me of what I wanted.
   [In this belief I have asserted the fact that the company is too complex to merit a single rating, evaluated its decision negatively and denied that it is a bad company.]

As these examples show, there are three parts to an acceptance belief. First, the author of the action under consideration is accepted as a fallible human being (in the case of myself and my supervisor) and as a complex whole (in the case of the company). Second, the action under consideration is rated (in each case negatively). Third, there is a statement negating the global negative rating of the person or institution.

Acceptance beliefs meet the four criteria for rationality. First, they are flexible. They recogise that organisms, institutions and life conditions are too complex to merit a single rating, although their different separate aspects can be evaluated legitimately. When I rate negatively my deficiencies that stopped me from being promoted, while accepting myself as a fallible human being with those deficiencies, I am using my evaluations flexibly. Thus, ratings are used flexibly in acceptance beliefs.

Second, they are logical. In acceptance beliefs, the parts are evaluated while the whole is accepted. A person's acceptance beliefs make sense because it is perfectly logical to assign a rating to a specific element that can be evaluated legitimately, and because it is not logical to assign a global rating to a complex entity with many different parts. When I rate my promotion-impeding deficiencies negatively, I am evaluating specific elements of my behaviour that can be legitimately rated. However, when I accept myself as a fallible human being, I refrain from assigning a global rating to a complex person who cannot be assigned such a rating.

Third, acceptance beliefs are consistent with reality. I can prove that I am a fallible human being with positive, negative and neutral aspects and I can prove that those deficiencies that blocked my promotion were negative.

Finally, acceptance beliefs promote goal achievement. If I accept myself as a fallible human being for my negatively evaluated job deficiencies, I am more likely to correct these deficiencies than if I were to condemn myself for having them in the first place. My self-accepting attitude will encourage me to focus on my deficiencies, and my negative ratings of these deficiencies will motivate me to endeavour to correct them.

As with the other two derivatives of preferential/desiring beliefs, the strength of my preference will have an impact on my acceptance belief derivative. The stronger my belief, the more negative my rating will be of my behaviour (in this case) that interferes with my preference being met and the harder it will be for me to accept myself as a fallible human being, although I will still be able to do this.

A final word on acceptance beliefs concerns the word acceptance. Many people, on hearing the word acceptance tend to think that it means resignation on the one hand and condoning on the other. In REP, acceptance has neither of these meanings. When I accept myself as a fallible human being who has negatively rated work deficiencies, I am not saying that I have to resign myself to the fact that I can do nothing about these deficiencies. Far from it. What I am saying is that while my essence as a human is fallibility, because humans can strive to improve their behaviour, I can do the same by focusing on my deficiencies, understanding them better and striving to improve my job perfomance by learning from my errors. Similarly, when I accept myself as a fallible human being for my work deficiencies I am not condoning these deficiencies. Rather, I am recognising that these deficiencies are negative in that they interfered with me obtaining my desired job promotion. Again, here as elsewhere, it is important to distinguish between words and their meanings in REP (Dryden, 1986).

Let me consider condemnation/downing beliefs. If I believe that I must get promotion, then I will tend to make the following condemnatory/downing conclusions: self-condemnation/downing; other-condemnation/downing; and condemning/downing life conditions. Let me consider these beliefs one at a time.

Self-condemnation/downing

If I think that the reason I failed to be promoted was because I was deficient at work, then I will tend to make a self-condemnatory conclusion which arises from my musturbatory belief. My full irrational belief will be along the following lines: 'I absolutely should have been promoted. The main reason I was not is, I see now, that I have been deficient at various aspects of my work. I absolutely shouldn't have been deficient in these respects and because I was this proves that I am no good.'

Note that I have two musturbatory beliefs here. The first, 'I absolutely should have been promoted' is my main must. Once I have attributed my failure to something – in this case my own work deficiencies – then it is very likely, not inevitable, that I will bring a musturbatory belief to this reason. As you will see this holds true for the other two condemnatory/downing beliefs that I discuss below. In this example, once I inferred that my work deficiencies were the cause of my failure to be promoted, then I demanded that I absolutely should not have such deficiencies. From this must I derive my self-condemnatory/downing belief: I am no good for having these work deficiencies.

Other-condemnation/downing

If I think that the reason I failed to be promoted was because my supervisor at work gave me an undeserved job appraisal, then I will tend to make another condemnatory conclusion from my musturbatory belief. My full irrational belief will be along the following lines: 'I absolutely should have been promoted. The main reason I was not is, I see now, that my supervisor unfairly gave me a negative job appraisal. She (in this case) absolutely shouldn't have done this to me and because she did this proves that she is no good'.

Again note that I have two musturbatory beliefs here. The first, 'I absolutely should have been promoted', is my main must. As I noted above, once I have attributed my failure to something – in this case my supervisor's unfair job appraisal – then it is very likely, although again not inevitable, that I will bring a musturbatory belief to this reason. In this example, once I inferred that my work supervisor's unfair job appraisal was the cause of my failure to be promoted, I demanded that she absolutely should not have given me such a report. From this must I derived my other-condemnatory/downing belief: She is no good for spoiling my chances of getting promotion.

Condemning/downing life conditions

If I think that the reason I failed to be promoted was due, for example, to the company changing its policy on promotions at the last moment (an example of impersonal life conditions), then I will tend to make a conclusion from my musturbatory belief in which I make a global condemnatory statement about a broad aspect of my life conditions. My full irrational belief will be along the following lines: "I absolutely should have been promoted. The main reason I was not is, I see now, that the company changed its policy on promotions at the last minute. It absolutely shouldn't have done this and because it did this proves that the company is no good.'

Note, yet again, that I have two musturbatory beliefs here. The first, 'I absolutely should have been promoted', is my main must. Once I have attributed my failure to the company's change of policy then it is very likely, although once again not inevitable, that I will bring a musturbatory belief to this reason. This is what in fact happened in this case. Once I inferred that the change of policy was the cause of my failure to be promoted, I demanded that it absolutely should not have done this. From this must I derived my condemnatory/ downing belief: The company is no good for changing its policy.

The defensive nature of some irrational beliefs

It is interesting to note that some irrational beliefs are defensive in nature because they serve to protect the individual from greater distress. Let me illustrate this by taking the example of the three condemnatory/downing beliefs just discussed. Let us assume that I hold the following irrational belief: 'I absolutely must achieve promotion and I am no good if I don't'.

You will recognise that this belief has two parts. The first part contains a musturbatory belief and the second part is a self-condemnatory belief which is derived from my must. When activated, this self-condemnatory belief leads to powerful disturbed emotions, such as depression, when it is clear that I have not been promoted. In order to protect myself from self-condemnation and the depression which in this case accompanies it, I need to find a reason to explain my failure other than my own deficits. One way that I can do this is to find evidence that another person has prevented me from being promoted.

When I say 'find evidence' I do not mean that I am knowingly looking for proof that another person has hindered my promotion prospects. Rather, this process of finding a reason for my failure, that can be attributed to another person most likely occurs outside of my awareness. If I cannot readily find clear-cut evidence that another person has hampered my promotion chances, I can scan past events and 'find' evidence consistent with the view that another person is responsible for my failure to be promoted. Again, I am not doing this knowingly. Thus, I am not overtly saying to myself: 'Now, unless I find that another person is responsible for my failure to be promoted, I will blame myself. Now there must be some evidence I can find. Let me see. Yes, didn't my supervisor...'. However, something like this is happening outside of my awareness and happening very rapidly when I employ other-condemnation as a defensive manoeuvre to protect myself from self-condemnation.

The same process occurs when I employ a condemnatory/downing belief directed towards a broad aspect of life conditions as a defence against self-condemnation. When this occurs in the example of my company changing its promotion policy, my condemnation of the company serves to prevent me from condemning myself for failing to gain promotion. This is not to say that I am not annoyed about the change in policy. Far from it; I would not condemn the company, however, if I did not need to defend myself against the self-condemnatory belief that otherwise would be activated.

How am I to know, for example, whether or not my other-condemnatory irrational belief is self-protective (or to use a psychological term, ego-defensive)? One way would be for me to ask myself: If I did not condemn the other person for stopping me from gaining promotion, would I condemn myself? If so, I would then need to ask myself: Psychologically, would I rather condemn the other person or myself? If the answer is the former then my other-condemnatory belief is probably defensive; if the answer is the latter then it is probably not defensive.

Beliefs exist at different levels of abstraction

In this section I consider the viewpoint that beliefs occur at different levels, and I discuss specific beliefs, general beliefs, core beliefs and philosophies.

Specific beliefs

So far, I have considered specific rational and specific irrational beliefs. These are beliefs that a person holds in a given situation. Thus, when I hold the irrational belief 'I must receive promotion at work', I am specifying the precise conditions about which I am thinking irrationally, i.e. a possible promotion. Note that this belief gives no clues concerning how I might think about others things in my life that I may desire.

Suppose that I want to be elected treasurer at my bowls club. Just because I hold an irrational belief about getting promotion at work does not mean that I hold an irrational belief about being elected club treasurer. It might; but it would be an unwarranted conclusion to assume that the existence of an irrational belief about one aspiration means the existence of an irrational belief about another. There may be many reasons why I might be thinking rationally about my aspiration at the bowls club. First, my desire about being elected bowls club treasurer may be weaker than my desire to be promoted at work. Albert Ellis has frequently made the point that we are much more likely to change our flexible desires into rigid musts when our desires are strong as apposed to when they are weak. Second, my two respective desires may be equally strong, but I may change only my work related desire into a must, while my recreation related desire remains a non-dogmatic wish. This may be due to many factors. The point that I wish to make is that musturbatory beliefs about one situation are in themselves poor predictors of the existence of such beliefs in other situations, even if the theme is the same. In the example I am considering, the theme that is common to both situations is advancement. It could be status or approval among others (see Figure 3.3); the point is that the person holding the belief is often the best judge of the relevant theme.

General beliefs

Let us suppose that my belief is more general. I believe that I must achieve advancement whenever I seek it at work. This belief is more general than my specific irrational belief about getting promoted. Indeed, it encompasses it. However, the more general belief should help predict how I think about other work situations that are related to the theme of advancement. Thus, I may hold the following specific beliefs:

1. I must get the bonus that I have asked for.
2. I must get onto the management training course that I have applied for.
3. When they move me from my present office they must give me a better room than they give to other people of my grade.

If my more general irrational belief holds true and the situations I have specified are examples of advancement at work, then the specific beliefs I have identified will also be irrational.

My irrational belief about advancement may be even more general. Thus, I may believe 'I must achieve advancement whenever I seek it'. This belief is more general than the belief that 'I must achieve advancement whenever I seek it at work', because it does not specify the conditions where the belief applies. Figure 3.3 shows the beliefs that I have discussed so far in ascending order of specificity.

Core beliefs

1. I must get promoted at work.

2. I must achieve advancement whenever I seek it at work.

3. I must achieve advancement whenever I seek it.

Figure 3.3. Irrational beliefs about advancement in ascending order of specificity.

Beliefs 2 and 3 are core if the theme of advancement occupies a fairly central place in this individual's personal domain.

The more general a person's irrational belief is, the more likely it is that the belief will be regarded as core, assuming that the belief is about an issue that is reasonably central in that individual's personal domain. Thus, irrational beliefs 2 and 3 in Figure 3.3 can be regarded as core if the theme of advancement occupies a fairly central place in my personal domain. Thus, according to REP (and using the example discussed above), a core irrational belief is an irrational belief that I hold about a central theme in my personal domain (in my case – advancement) across a broad range of situations specified in the belief (at work in belief 2 or in all advancevent situations in belief 3).

How core a person's irrational belief is depends on the co-existence of two factors: (1) how general the belief is; and (2) how central the theme is in the individual's personal domain. Thus, the more core a person's irrational belief, the more general it is and the more centrally placed in the individual's personal domain is the theme of the belief. Thus, if advancement was of central importance to me and I believed that I must gain it in all or a large number of significant situations where I seek it, then my irrational belief is core. Although I have been using irrational beliefs in these examples to demonstrate the difference between specific, general and core irrational beliefs, the same points can be made about rational beliefs as shown in Figure 3.4.

So far I have only discussed one theme – advancement – in discussing specific, general and core beliefs. What other themes are there? Themes that regularly feature in people's descriptions of their prob-

1. I would like to gain promotion, but I do not have to do so.

2. I would like to achieve advancement whenever I seek it at work, but I do not have to do so.

3. I would like to achieve advancement whenever I seek it, but I do not have to do so.

Figure 3.4. Rational beliefs about advancement in ascending order of specificity.

Beliefs 2 and 3 are core if the theme of advancement occupies a fairly central place in this individual's personal domain.

lems as they recount them in counselling and psychotherapy are shown in Figure 3.5. This is not an exhaustive list and it is idiosyncratic because it is taken from one person's practice (my own). However, it does demonstrate what are the themes that people are preoccupied with, and as such constitutes a reasonable guide to themes that are likely to be personally significant. As with the theme of advancement, each of the themes mentioned in Figure 3.5 may provide the content for specific beliefs, general beliefs and core beliefs.

Philosophies

As discussed above, when an irrational belief is general, it occurs in a large number of situations where the person's theme is a feature. Thus, when my irrational belief about advancement is general, specific examples of this belief will be activated in a large number of situations where advancement is salient. In particular, I am more likely to be disturbed if there is a good chance that I will not achieve the advancement that I am demanding, or if there is a good chance of losing the advancement that I have already gained.

Philosophies differ from general beliefs in that they encompass groups of themes. Thus, if I have an irrational philosophy about the broad area of affiliation, I may hold the following general irrational beliefs about other people (see Figure 3.5):

1. I must be loved by significant others.
2. I must be appreciated by significant others.
3. I must be approved of by significant others.

My corresponding rational philosophy about affiliation would comprise the following general rational beliefs:

1. I would like to be loved by significant others, but they do not have to love me.

Themes related to self

1. Behaviour
Achieving	[Achievement]
Performing competently	[Competence]
Acting morally	[Morality]
Living up to one's own standards	[Standards]
Being strong	[Strength]

2. Conditions
Maintaining a sense of comfort	[Comfort]
Achieving a desired rank or position	[Status]
Gaining power and influence	[Power]
Being able to be autonomous	[Autonomy]
Being in control	[Control]
Having certainty	[Certainty]
Striving for fulfillment	[Fulfillment]

Themes related to others

1. Affiliation
Being accepted by significant others	[Acceptance]
Being approved of by significant others	[Approval]
Being loved by significant others	[Love]
Having one's contributions appreciated	[Appreciation]
Being able to trust significant others	[Trust]

2. Conditions
Being treated fairly	[Fairness]
Receiving justice	[Justice]

Figure 3.5. Examples of Personally Significant Themes

2. I want to be appreciated by significant others, but they do not have to appreciate me.
3. I want to be approved of by significant others, but they do not have to approve of me.

How many general beliefs comprise a philosophy? Although there is no agreed definitive view on this issue, my opinion is as follows. A group of general beliefs can be called a philosophy when that group contains at least 50 per cent of all possible beliefs in that area. Thus, in the examples just given, my group of general beliefs about affiliation in relation to others constitutes a philosophy because that group includes 60 per cent of all possible general beliefs in the area of affiliation (see Figure 3.5).

As I discuss more fully later (see pp.82-87), Albert Ellis argues that there are two major areas of psychological disturbance: ego disturbance (disturbance related to my beliefs about myself); and discomfort disturbance (disturbance related to my beliefs about the broad area of discomfort). If I have an irrational philosophy in the area of ego disturbance, then I will frequently hold self-condemnatory beliefs in most of the personally significant themes where judgments about the self is possible. By contrast, if I hold self-accepting beliefs in those same themes, then I can be said to have a rational philosophy in the area of ego health.

If we combine my ego-related and discomfort-related beliefs, we can say that I have a general irrational philosophy if most of my specific and general (core) beliefs, which are related to personally significant themes, are irrational, while if most of these beliefs are rational we can say that I have a general rational philosophy.

Ellis refers to a general rational philosophy as an elegant philosophy. In an interview with Steve Weinrach (1980), Albert Ellis referred to a super-elegant (rational) philosophy. A person who held such a philosophy would think rationally in the vast majority of his or her life and would rarely make him- or herself about anything. To help people strive towards such a super-elegant philosophy, Ellis (1990) wrote a book with an intriguing title: *'How to Stubbornly Refuse to Make Yourself Disturbed about Anything – Yes Anything!!'*. Ellis is realistic enough to know that few, if any of us, will reach such lofty heights – at least for long. However, that fact, he believes, should not detract from our efforts to acquire rational beliefs in as many areas of our life as we can.

Having dealt with the area of beliefs in some detail, I now consider ABC's and the principle of emotional responsibility.

Chapter 4
ABC's and the principle of emotional responsibility

At the end of Chapter 1, I briefly introduced the ABC model of psychological functioning. In Chapter 2, I thoroughly discussed A (which stands for activating events and includes the events themselves and the interpretations and inferences that we form about these events). Then, in Chapter 3, I considered B (which stands for the evaluative beliefs that we hold about A). C stands for the emotional and behavioural consequences that stem from the beliefs we hold at B. In this chapter I will deal more extensively with the ABC's of REP, and focus on emotional C's while dealing with the principle of emotional responsibilty. This principle is a central idea in rational-emotive psychology.

The ABC's of 'heartache'

In 1993, an American woman won a large sum of money in damages from a man to whom she was engaged. The woman claimed that the man had promised her a 'great adventure', but broke off the engagement after seven weeks. The woman sued for her hurt feelings and was awarded US$178 000 in consideration of her heartbreak and the cost of her subsequent psychiatric counselling.

It is important to note that this man was not merely held responsible for his own behaviour. A jury of seven men and one woman in Illinois decided that he was also responsible for his ex-fiancee's feelings. In doing so, they were saying that A (in this case, the abrupt breaking of the engagement) directly caused C (the woman's heartache). In REP, this is known as the 'A causes C' model of emotions. This model, which denies the effect that our beliefs have on our feelings, is unfortunately widely held in our society. You simply have to listen casually to people's conversations to hear A-C language. An illustrative list of common A-C statements can be found in Figure 4.1.

He made me so angry.

That made me depressed.

My mother makes me feel so guilty.

Tests always make me anxious.

He was trying to make me jealous.

My son brought shame on the family.

Figure 4.1. Common A-C statements.

As all of the statements in Figure 4.1 make it clear that our emotions are deemed to be caused by outside events. These statements absolve us from any responsibility for our emotions. Therefore, we can blame our feelings either on events that happen to us or on how other people treat us. When we are questioned on the validity of this model of emotions, we reply to the effect that if the events at A had not happened then we would not have felt the way we did. They did happen, however, we did experience the feelings, and thus the events caused our emotions. This model is presented in diagrammatic form in Figure 4.2.

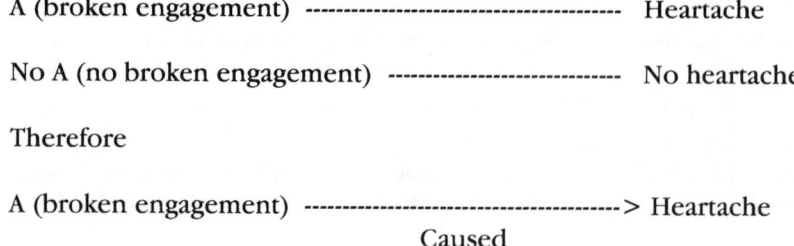

A (broken engagement) -- Heartache

No A (no broken engagement) ------------------------------ No heartache

Therefore

A (broken engagement) --> Heartache
                                            Caused

Figure 4.2. Argument used to justify A causes C model.

This argument, however, is basically flawed in that it does not distinguish between correlation (the co-existence of A and C) and causation (the presence of A causes C). Simply because the presence of an A (e.g. man breaking engagement) co-exists with an emotional C (e.g. heartache) does not mean that A caused C even if the absence of the A (no broken engagement) co-exists with the absence of an emotional C (no heartache).

This reasoning neglects the fact that another factor (let us call this B) could cause C or that C is a product of an interaction between A and B, or that the product of a complex interaction of variables may include A and B. The position taken by rational-emotive psychologists is that the way I feel (C) about an event (A) is, at the most simplest level of analysis, the product of an interaction between the event (actual, interpreted or inferred) and my belief (rational or irrational) about that event. Indeed, if we were to take an even more detailed look at this phenomenon, we would see that my emotion at C is a product of a complex relationship between A, B and a number of other variables (including prior level of emotionality, tiredness, beliefs about how I should feel in such circumstances, etc.)

As this book is designed to be an invitation to rational-emotive psychology, I will consider and explore the simple A×B → C model. (I give, however, a flavour of the intricacy of REP in Chapter 8 where I consider the complex interactions between A's, B's and C's.) Figure 4.3 provides a diagrammatic account of the A×B → C explanation of the broken engagement – heartache example.

A (broken engagement)----------------------------------- Heartache

No A (no broken engagement)-------------------------- No heartache

A (broken engagement) x B (belief) ----------------> Heartache

Figure 4.3. A × B → C explanation.

The position that I take, therefore, is that to understand the way a person feels, at the very least, we need to understand the object of that emotion (especially the person's inferences), and his or her beliefs about the object, and the inferences made about it. In reality, because there are a number of other variables involved (see above) that I do not discuss here, we cannot use causative language. Thus, I do not consider that beliefs cause emotions; nor do I think that our emotions are caused by our inferences and beliefs taken together. My position is that inferences and beliefs are at the core of our emotions and in order to understand a person's emotions we need to understand the inferences that he or she makes and the beliefs that he or she holds.

Let me apply this position to the broken engagement-heartache example. Although I do not know the precise details I will speculate on the inferences and beliefs of the jilted woman to demonstrate that the jury did not give her responsibility for her own emotions. Let us assume both that the man concerned did promise her a 'great adventure' and that she believed him, how can we understand this woman's hurt and heartache? Figure 4.4 offers one explanation by putting her experience in ABC terms.

A: Broken engagement (Actual A)
'I've been very badly let down and treated in a manner that I did not deserve' (A as inference)

B: 1. He absolutely should not have treated me in this way.

2. It is awful that I have been treated in this way. Poor me!

3. I can't stand the fact that I have been treated in this very bad manner.

C: Hurt

Figure 4.4. ABC of jilted woman's hurt

As can be shown from Figure 4.4, I have included under A the actual event (broken engagement) and the aspect of the situation about which the woman was hurt most ('I've been very badly let down and treated in a manner that I did not deserve'). This serves as the critical A. Note that at this point the woman is mainly disturbed about 'being let down' and 'treated in a manner that I did not deserve'. Whether or not it is true that she has been let down and treated in an undeserved fashion is not the point in understanding her emotional experience. For her, it is true and that is the critical A. However, as I emphasised in Chapter 3, inferences on their own do not fully account for a person's emotions. Though partly evaluative, this woman's inference does not contain sufficient evaluative information for us to determine her affective response. She could evaluate, for example, this negatively inferred A in three main ways: using rational beliefs, irrational beliefs or beliefs signifying indifference. If she held indifference-type beliefs about the inferred event, then she would not experience any significant emotion about the way she was treated. We know, however, that she felt great hurt so we can eliminate beliefs signifying indifference from our enquiry.

How are we to know whether her beliefs are rational or irrational? One method would be to ask the woman directly. The problem with this approach is that her beliefs are likely to be implicit and therefore out of her awareness. She may not be able to identify them spontaneously in response to our enquiry. In addition, even if she did answer our question, she would probably come up with alternative phrasings of her inferences rather than her beliefs. Most often people do not know the difference between beliefs and inferences and do not reliably identify beliefs when they are asked to do so. Consequently, we need to have a framework which posits the existence of specific types of inferences and beliefs when a person experiences particular emotions.

It is one of rational-emotive psychology's unique contributions to psychology that it provides such a framework. In Chapter 5, I summarise this framework and in Chapter 7 I apply it to different emotional states. For the present, and returning to our example, we need to know what beliefs are associated with hurt. REP hypothesises that hurt is an unconstructive negative emotion that is based on a set of irrational beliefs. Applying this to our example, we see from Figure 4.4 that the woman holds a number of irrational beliefs:

1. 'He absolutely should not have treated me in this way.'
2. 'It is awful that I have been treated in this way. Poor me!'
3. 'I can't stand the fact that I have been treated in this very bad manner.'

REP predicts that if the woman held a set of rational beliefs about the same inferred A then she would have experienced a constructive negative emotion called disappointment (see Figure 4.5). As discussed in Chapter 2, the stronger her rational beliefs about being let down and badly treated, the more intense her feeling of disappointment is likely to be. However, even strong constructive negative feelings are qualitatively different from unconstructive negative feelings.

- A. Broken engagement (Actual A)
  'I've been very badly let down and treated in a manner that I did not deserve.' (A as inference)

- B. 1. It would have been highly desirable that he had not treated me in this way, but there is no law of the universe to decree that he absolutely should not have done so.

    2. It is bad that I have been treated in this way, but not awful. I am not "Poor me!", even though I am in a poor situation.

    3. I can stand the fact that I have been treated in this very bad manner, even though I will never like it.

- C. Strong Disappointment

Figure 4.5. ABC of jilted woman's disappointment

Thus, at the core of negative emotions (such as hurt and disappointment) is a set of inferences and beliefs. You will note that what distinguishes disappointment (i.e. the constructive negative emotion) from hurt (i.e. the unconstructive negative emotion) is not the inference that the person makes, but the belief about the inference. Thus, although we need to ascertain a person's inference and belief in understanding his or her specific emotion, the way in which we determine whether that negative emotion is healthy or unhealthy is by keenly differentiating his or her rational beliefs from his or her irrational beliefs.

Emotional responsibility

Having discussed the example of the jilted woman and presented an ABC of both her actual emotional response to being jilted (i.e. hurt) and her possible emotional response to it (i.e. disappointment), let me return to the issue of emotional responsibility. My position would be that the man is responsible for his behaviour i.e. for breaking off the engagement after promising the woman a great adventure. He is responsible further for how he told her that their relationship was over. He cannot be held responsible, however, for her emotional response to this news. As my analysis clearly shows, the woman's emotional response (i.e. her hurt or, as she called it, her heartache) clearly stemmed from the inferences that she made and the beliefs that she held about the activating event. As these are her inferences and her beliefs they fall within her purview and, therefore, she is basically responsible for them.

Some people would argue, however, that her inference was correct: that the man did let her down badly and treat in a manner she did not deserve. Let us assume that her inference was indeed correct. This means that the man needs to take responsiblity for acting in the manner so described. Even under these these circumstances, however he is not responsible for her hurt (nor heartache). Her feelings of hurt stemmed mainly from the beliefs she held about this behaviour. She is therefore primarily responsible for her feelings of hurt because she is primarily responsible for the beliefs she holds.

You will note that the woman was awarded damages for her hurt feelings and not for being badly treated. If the damages had been awarded for how she was treated then that would have made sense because the man properly can be held responsible for his behaviour. In awarding the woman damages for her hurt feelings, the jury was operating on an 'A causes C' model of emotions. They decided that the man was responsible both for his behaviour and for the woman's feelings. Thus, they decreed that the woman was not responsible for her own emotions. In doing so they violated the principle of emotional responsibility: A person is largely responsible for his or her own feelings due to the beliefs that he or she holds about the event in question.

Objections to the principle of emotional responsibilty

The principle of emotional responsibility has been criticised in a number of respects: (1) it trivialises obnoxious activating events; (2) it blames the victim; (3) it does not apply when a person acts knowing that the other person concerned will be disturbed and (4) it does not apply when A is very bad or tragic.

Objection 1: Emotional responsibility trivialises obnoxious A's

It is argued that the principle of emotional responsibility leads to the trivialisation of obnoxious acts or deeds at A. If we hold the person responsible for her feelings are we not in some way lessening the gravity of these acts? The answer is a resounding 'no'. Merely because I hold the woman largely responsible for her feelings about the broken engagement does not mean that I consider the man's behaviour less bad than I would if I shared the jury's 'A causes C' model. In both cases, the man's actions are exactly the same. I do admit that giving the woman responsibility for her feelings may, in some, or even most, people's eyes, lessen the gravity of the man's behaviour. If the majority of people think that an illogical conclusion makes sense, however, this consensus does not make the conclusion any more logical.

A different version of the same criticism is that if we do not blame the man for how the woman feels, or, at the very least, hold him totally responsible for her feelings, then we are excusing or even condoning his behaviour. This criticism cannot be upheld for similar reasons as discussed above. Holding the woman largely responsible for her own feelings does not detract from the degree of badness of the man's actions. In addition, this criticism falls down because it implies 'black or white' thinking: either we take the extreme position of holding the man fully responsible for the woman's feelings or we are excusing or even condoning his actions. I hope you can now see that we can hold the woman largely responsible for her feelings and hold the man largely responsible for his actions, which we neither seek to excuse nor condone.

Objection 2: Emotional responsibility leads to blaming the victim

This 'black or white' form of reasoning is present in the second criticism of the emotional responsibility principle – blaming the victim.

Applying this to the present example, if we hold the woman responsible for her feelings, we are blaming her for her plight. In response, it is important to recognise that there is a world of difference between responsibility and blame. Responsibility assigns authorship to a behaviour, belief or feeling, whereas blame assigns a global negative rating of the person having responsibility for the behaviour, belief or feeling. Thus, if we were actually blaming the victim (in this case, the woman who experienced a broken engagement), we would first hold her responsible for her feelings – which we are doing; we would then hold her responsible for her plight – which we are not doing because the man was the one who broke the engagement, not the woman; finally we would blame or condemn the woman for being in the plight in which she found herself – which we are obviously not doing. In other words, by saying that the woman is largely resonsible for her feelings, we are saying nothing more than that. In doing so, we are seeking neither to absolve the man of his responsibilty for his own actions nor to ascribe blame to either party.

Objection 3: The principle cannot be applied when a person acts knowing that the other will be disturbed about the action

The third criticism is a more serious one. It asks the question whether someone is reponsible for another person's feelings if the person acts in a certain way knowing that the other will be disturbed as a result. Applying this question to our example: if the man knew that the woman would be very hurt about the break-up of their engagement, would he be responsible for her resultant hurt feelings? The answer to this question again is 'no'. Knowing that the woman would be hurt about the end of their relationship means that it is advisable for the man to break the news to her in a humane a manner as possible, i.e his additional responsibility is to be as sensitive as he can be to her feelings. If she predictably responds with hurt, then at least he has not added to her burden by being rude and insensitive to her feelings.

What if he did not show sensitivity and ended the relationship in a crass and brutal manner? Surely under such conditions it can be said that he made her feel hurt and was responsible both for this heartache and for the additional disturbed feelings that she would experience about the way in which he ended their relationship? The answer would still, ultimately, be 'no', although we are entering into even more tricky waters here. If he knew that she would be hurt and deliberately acted in a cruel and heartless manner while telling her that he was ending their relationship, then he is responsible both for the break-up of their engagement and for the way in which he did it. If he told her sensitively then he was constraining her choice of emotional response. As shown in Figures 4.4 and 4.5, the woman has a choice to respond with constructive disappointment or unconstructive hurt. His behaviour, even when sensitively and caringly executed, therefore limits her choice to two negative emotions. However, she still has a choice. She could, theoretically, choose to feel disappointed and is therefore responsible for this choice.

If he is insensitive and rude in the way he handles ending their relationship, he is making it harder for her to respond with disappointment rather than hurt and he ought to take responsibility for making it harder to respond healthily. She still has the choice to respond with disappointment, however, even if it is harder for her to do so and is thus still responsible for her own feelings in this context.

I want to stress two points here. First, saying that the woman is responsible for her feelings does not mean that the man can absolve himself from his responsibility for the fact of breaking off their engagement, or how he did it. He cannot hide behind a statement such as, 'She is responsible for her feelings, therefore the way she feels has nothing to do with me.' This statement is a complete cop-out and denies the fact that his behaviour contributes to her feelings, even though it does not cause them.

Second, the fact that the woman is responsible for her feelings does not mean that she can easily change them. It means that she has the choice to do so and that she can be helped to implement that choice. Saying that she has no responsibility for her feelings, is, in fact, a dismal message. It means that she has no choice but to feel disturbed about the end of the relationship, that she is a passive victim at the mercy of how the man has treated her and that she cannot change. By depriving her of responsibililty for her own emotions, this viewpoint ultimately dehumanises her.

Before we leave this particular criticism of the principle of emotional responsibility, I want to discuss a tendency among some of its critics to offer two incompatible viewpoints. On the one hand, they would say that the woman is responsible for her emotions, but on the other hand they would claim that the man can still be said to have hurt her feelings, particularly if he ended the relationship in a callous manner. What these critics seem to be saying is that the woman has responsibility for her emotions under favourable conditions, but relinquishes that responsibility when faced with very negative activating events.

While I have argued that the woman, in our example, is more likely to disturb herself about the broken engagement if the man is insensitive to her feelings, this does not mean that she relinquishes all of her emotional responsibility. What it does mean is that it is harder for her to implement this responsibility when faced with the fact of the broken engagement and the callous way in which the man ended their relationship. The man is responsible for the events that make it harder for her to implement responsibility for her emotions, but ultimately he is not responsible for taking that responsibility away from her entirely.

Objection 4: The principle does not apply when A is very bad or tragic

This latter point (above) is also my defence against the final attack on the principle of emotional responsibility, which, I admit, is the most difficult to answer and which makes the respondent sound insensitive when giving the response. I would argue, however, that the answer is not insensitive; rather, it is empowering. The criticism is this: how can a man (in this case) be said to be responsible for his emotions when he has been raped, for example. Surely under such tragic circumstances, we can say that the rapist did cause the man's disturbed feelings by raping him and that to say anything else is grossly insensitive and insulting to the man concerned.

Let me begin to respond to this point by making it quite clear that I do not condone the act of rape. I regard it as a hideous crime which should not go unpunished. Second, the distress experienced by almost all those who have been raped is, I believe, a normal and, in many ways, healthy response to this terrible event. Such distress is based on the idea that it is tragic to be violated in this manner and that it was very wrong for it to have occurred. Since this idea reflects the reality of the event and leads to very distressing, but healthy, feelings, then to this extent the rapist can be held responsible for the man's feelings. Nevertheless, however difficult it is for the man who has been raped to acknowledge, he may bring ideas to the event which are not an intrinsic part of the event, but which lead to additional disturbed feelings. In other words, the man is responsible for these disturbed feelings because he brings ideas to the rape that are not an intrinsic part of it. I do recognise that it is easy for the man to bring such ideas and that he cannot realistically be expected to challenge them soon after the violation. However, by the very fact that he brings these ideas to the violation, he is responsible for them and for the disturbed feelings that are associated with them. By saying this, I am not saying that the man should be blamed for bringing these ideas to the event, nor am I advocating that this should in any way lessen the sentence that the rapist should receive under the law.

By claiming that the man is responsible for the ideas that he brings to the experience and for the associated disturbed feelings, I conclude that, at the right time, he can challenge and change these ideas, thereby ensuring that he does not add unconstructive disturbed feelings to constructive distressed feelings. To say that these additional ideas are part of the rape implies that the man will experience disturbed feelings for longer.

What are some of the ideas that the man may bring to the rape that will lead to disturbed as well as distressd feelings? Here are four:

1. This has completely ruined my life.
2. I am now completely worthless.
3. I'm bad because I absolutely should have prevented it.
4. The rapist spotted a weakness in me and I absolutely should not have this weakness.

Let us take the first two ideas and let me explain why I think that the man who was raped is responsible for them and the disturbed feelings they engender.

1. 'This has completely ruined my life.'

There is no denying that, for almost everybody, rape is a very tragic event. It cannot be condoned and the perpetrator, if caught and found guilty, ideally should receive a heavy prison sentence and remedial treatment. Rape is an act that changes lives. However, it is not in itself an event that ruins lives. If this idea is brought, then it will lead to needless disturbance. The person who brings that idea to the event needs to take responsibility for it and for the disturbed emotions that this idea fosters. In doing so, he can begin to see that the idea is not an intrinsic and lasting part of rape and can be changed at a suitable point in the healing process.

2. 'I am now completely worthless.'

The same argument holds true for this belief. If it were true that rape can make a person completely worthless, then anyone who has ever been raped is therefore worthless. This is a preposterous notion. What the person is doing here is wildly over-generalising from one healthy idea – I've come through a tragic experience – to a second unhealthy idea – therefore I am now completely worthless. Again, the person who contributes that idea needs to take responsibility for it and for the disturbed emotions that the belief engenders. If he can do this he again can acknowledge that this belief is not an inevitable and ongoing part of rape and can thus be changed, at the relevant time.

To summarise, rape is a tragic occurrence which, no matter how rationally one thinks about it, will lead to great emotional distress on the part of the person who is raped. This is natural and healthy in that it reflects the negativity of the experience, helps the person to adjust to it and, eventually, to move on. When a person brings to the event of rape beliefs that lead to emotional disturbance, however, then that person is responsible for that addition, no matter how understandable it is that he (or she) may think that way. Regarding the person as responsible in this way does not mean that we condone rape or minimise its negative effects; nor does it mean that we 'blame the victim'. Indeed we are empowering the person because he comes to realise that although distress is an inevitable part of rape, disturbance is not, and that he can do something to prevent becoming disturbed about it – namely, to take responsibility for the beliefs that he brings to the event which are not an intrinsic part of it and thence challenge and change them. Not giving the person responsibility for his disturbed emotions in this case means that he is less likely to challenge and change the ideas that underpin these feelings.

Having dealt with the thorny principle of emotional responsibility rather extensively, we are now in a position to deal with other important aspects of our emotions and I consider these in the next chapter.

Chapter 5
Emotions

As I discussed in Chapter 4, emotions in rational–emotive psychology are deemed to be based mainly on the inferences and evaluations that we make of actual activating events. In this chapter, I consider this point in some detail. In particular, I distinguish between constructive and unconstructive negative emotions, point out that we often experience a mixture of emotions, and I also discuss the concept of 'false' emotions and why we may exaggerate our unconstructive, negative emotions.

Unconstructive and constructive negative emotions

I mentioned in the previous chapter that a person's emotions are based, in large part, on the inferences that the person makes about an actual activating event and the beliefs that the person holds about these inferences. REP has been derived from a therapeutic method and as such it focuses mainly on negative emotions. In doing so, it makes an important distinction between two types of negative emotions: constructive negative emotions and unconstructive negative emotions. These two types of emotions differ in one important respect: constructive negative emotions stem from rational beliefs; whereas unconstructive negative emotions stem from irrational beliefs. Let me illustrate this by giving another example.

Rex, a 26-year-old man, is about to take his driving test and is very anxious about this. Figure 5.1 presents an ABC analysis of Rex's anxiety, an emotion deemed to be an unconstructive negative emotion by REP.

As Figure 5.1 shows, Rex's anxiety about taking and possibly failing his driving test stems from two irrational beliefs: (1) I must pass my driving test; and (2) If I fail my driving test it will prove I'm an idiot.

A: I might fail my driving test.

B: 1. I must pass my driving test.

2. If I fail my driving test it will prove I'm an idiot.

C: Anxiety

Figure 5.1. ABC of Rex's driving test anxiety.

Compare this with an ABC analysis of Rex's concern about taking his driving test, an emotion deemed to be a constructive negative emotion by REP (see Figure 5.2).

As Figure 5.2 shows, Rex's concern about taking and possibly failing his driving test stems from two rational beliefs: (1) I want to pass my driving test, but I don't have to do so; and (2) If I fail my driving test, I can still accept myself as a fallible human being. I would not be an idiot.

It is important to note that the difference between Rex's anxiety and concern lies in the fact that his beliefs are irrational in anxiety, yet rational in concern. His inferences are the same in both cases. Thus, one way in which unconstructive negative emotions differ from constructive negative emotions concerns the content of the beliefs that underpin them – irrational in the case of the former and rational in the case of the latter.

A second manner in which unconstructive negative emotions differ from those that are constructive concerns the consequences of the emotions themselves. Thus, anxiety is an unconstructive negative emotion in that it has more negative than positive consequences. While anxiety is energising, it tends to lead the person to focus on how well or poorly he is doing rather than on what he is actually doing.

A: I might fail my driving test.

B: 1. I want to pass my driving test, but I don't have to do so.

2. If I fail my driving test, I can still accept myself as a fallible human being. I would not be an idiot.

C: Concern

Figure 5.2. ABC of Rex's concern about taking his driving test.

Consequently, it will tend to increase rather than decrease errors. In addition, anxiety tends to lead the person to focus on what could go wrong rather than what could go right. As such it increases the chances that the person will make mistakes. Put differently, anxiety leads the person to have task–irrelevant thoughts rather than task–relevant thoughts, and this is coupled with the increasing impairment of concentration and skilled performance.

In Rex's case, his anxiety will lead him to focus on how well (or strictly speaking, how poorly) he is driving rather than on what he needs to do in order to drive well. It will increase his tendency to focus on thoughts which will impede his driving ability, such as 'What if I stall the engine', 'I am not looking in the mirror frequently enough', 'I won't be prepared when the examiner wants me to make an emergency stop', and 'I'm not driving well at all'.

By contrast, concern is a constructive negative emotion because it has more positive than negative consequences. Like anxiety, concern is energising, but it tends to lead the person to focus on what he is doing rather than on how well he is doing it. Consequently, it will tend to decrease rather than increase errors. In addition, concern tends to lead the person to focus on what could go right rather than what could go wrong. As such it decreases the chances that the person will make mistakes. Put differently, concern leads the person to have task–relevant thoughts rather than task–irrelevant thoughts with the increasing likelihood of increased concentration and skilled performance.

In Rex's case, his concern will lead him to focus on what he needs to do to drive well rather than on how well or how poorly he is driving. It will decrease his tendency to focus on thoughts that will impede his driving ability, and will encourage him to make short, constructive self–instructions to guide his driving performance, such as 'Look in the mirror', 'Change up a gear now', 'Indicate left', and 'Focus!'.

A third way in which unconstructive negative emotions differ from constructive negative emotions concerns the internal experience of these emotions. Unconstructive negative emotions tend to be experienced as more aversive than those that are constructive, even if the level of intensity of both types of emotion is the same. Thus, if Rex is very anxious about taking his driving test, he is more likely to experience this state as being more aversive than if he was equally very concerned, but not anxious. This is one reason why people tend to seek counselling or psychotherapy more frequently for their strong unconstructive negative emotions than for their strong constructive negative emotions. Another reason for this differential help–seeking has been discussed above, i.e. unconstructive negative emotions tend to be more disruptive of performance than constructive negative emotions.

Constructive and unconstructive negative emotions are qualitatively different

Many therapists sensibly ask their clients what they want to achieve from therapy. This helps both client and therapist to be goal-oriented and encourages both to be focused on the work that needs to be done for the client to achieve his or her goals. As I have said, many clients come to therapy seeking help for their unconstructive negative emotions. When these clients are asked what they want to gain from therapy, many of them state that they wish to experience a decrease in intensity of their major unconstructive negative emotion. Thus, if asked for his therapeutic goal, Rex might say that he wants to feel 'less anxious' about his driving test and many therapists would accept this as a helpful and legitimate goal. However, from a rational–emotive psychology perspective, this goal is problematic. Let us take Rex's case to illustrate this point.

As you will recall, Rex's anxiety stems from the following irrational beliefs that he holds about possibly failing his driving test: (1) I must pass my driving test; and (2) If I fail my driving test it will prove I'm an idiot. The greater that Rex's conviction is in these irrational ideas, the more anxious he will feel. Thus, if he is helped to feel less anxious about the prospect of failing his driving test, in effect he is being helped to lessen his conviction in his irrational beliefs. But, and this is the point, he will still hold them.

If, on the other hand he is helped to challenge and change these irrational beliefs and is encouraged to develop conviction in the following rational beliefs: (1) I want to pass my driving test, but I don't have to do so, and (2) If I fail my driving test, I can still accept myself as a fallible human being. I would not be an idiot – then, he would not be less anxious; rather, he would be unanxious, but concerned about failing. Moreover, the stronger that Rex's conviction is in these rational beliefs, the stronger will be his feelings of concern.

What rational–emotive psychology argues, then, is that constructive and unconstructive negative emotions should be placed on two different continua. Other approaches to psychology do not differentiate between these unconstructive and constructive emotions, and, hence, they tend to fuse these different types of emotions and put them on a single continuum. Figures 5.3 and 5.4 summarise these two different positions.

In Figure 5.3, anxiety and concern are undifferentiated. As such the continuum does not allow for someone to be strongly concerned, but, at the same time, unanxious. Also, the view implicit in this single continuum explanation of anxiety and concern is that moderate or mild negative feelings are healthy and that strong and intense negative feelings are unhealthy.

```
X ------------- X ------------- X ------------ X ---------- X
   No             Mild          Moderate        Strong        Intense
 anxiety         anxiety         anxiety        anxiety       anxiety
   or              or              or             or             or
 concern         concern         concern        concern       concern
```

Figure 5.3. Single continuum showing no differentiation between anxiety and concern

Continuum 1: Anxiety – based on irrational beliefs

```
X ------------- X ------------- X ------------ X ---------- X
   No             Mild          Moderate        Strong        Intense
 anxiety         anxiety         anxiety        anxiety       anxiety
```

Continuum 2: Concern – based on rational beliefs

```
X ------------- X ------------- X ------------ X ---------- X
   No             Mild          Moderate        Strong        Intense
 concern         concern         concern        concern       concern
```

Figure 5.4. Two continua showing differentiation between anxiety and concern.

By contrast, Figure 5.4 – which puts forward the REP view of constructive and unconstructive negative emotions – does differentiate between anxiety and concern and thus does allow for someone to feel strong or intense concern without any anxiety. REP allows for this because it posits two continua, one that is based on rational beliefs and the other that is based on irrational beliefs. According to this view, constructive negative emotions stem from rational beliefs and can be mild, moderate, strong or even intense, while unconstructive negative emotions stem from irrational beliefs and can also be mild, moderate, strong and intense.

Rational–emotive psychology also argues that people can change their healthy rational beliefs into unhealthy irrational beliefs, especially when their rational beliefs are strong (see Chapter 3). For example, if Rex holds the strong rational belief 'I really want to pass my driving test', he is more likely to change this to '...and therefore I have to pass it', than if he holds the weaker rational belief 'I want, to some degree, to pass my driving test'. Thus, if Rex, in this case, is very concerned to pass his driving test, he is more likely (but not inevitably) to go on to feel anxious about the test than if his concern was moderate or even mild. I say that it is not inevitable that Rex will go on to be anxious about passing his driving test if his concern about it is very strong because he could always believe 'I really want to pass my driving, but I do not have to do so'. Because people fairly easily change their rational beliefs into irrational beliefs, we can discern only when a belief is rational if it is expressed in its full form, which in Rex's case is 'I really want to pass my driving test, but I do not have to do so'. Consequently, we can only tell if Rex is concerned and not anxious about taking his driving test by similarly inspecting the full form of his belief.

When someone experiences an unconstructive negative emotion, there is often (but not always) the germ of a constructive negative emotion in his or her experience. Thus, when Rex experiences anxiety about taking his driving test, it is because he is thinking irrationally about it. However, it is probable that he also has a rational belief about taking his test, i.e. he wants to pass it. Thus, the germ of concern is present in Rex's experience when he is anxious. This point is important because if we were to help Rex give up his irrational beliefs about his driving test and become unanxious about it, he would still be concerned about it because only his rational beliefs remain. We would not have to help him invent a set of rational beliefs about the test, because this set would already be in place. We would need to help Rex strengthen his conviction in his rational beliefs, however, but this is an entirely different matter to that of helping him create these beliefs from scratch. This explains why if Rex truly wishes to pass his driving test he would still be constructively concerned about passing it once we have helped him to become unanxious about it. I say constructively concerned here because, as discussed above, Rex's feelings of concern would motivate him to do well and facilitate his concentration during the test.

I mentioned earlier that when someone experiences an unconstructive negative emotion, there is often (but not always) the germ of a constructive negative emotion in his or her experience. Let me give an example when this is not the case. Let us suppose that Rex is afraid of incurring his father's disapproval and that his father insists on Rex learning to drive even though Rex has no interest in so doing. In this scenario, Rex might believe that he must pass his driving test without the accompanying desire to do so. Helping Rex to rid himself of his musturbatory belief about passing the test will not, in this instance, lead him to want to do so. The real issue here for Rex is not related to passing the driving test, it is related to incurring his father's displeasure.

Indifference: often sought, rarely constructive

I mentioned at the beginning of the previous section that when asked about their therapeutic goals, clients in counselling often say that they wish to feel less of an unconstructive negative emotion. I explained why this would pose problems for rational–emotive psychologists in that achieving this would mean that (1) these people would still hold irrational beliefs (albeit in a weaker form) and (2) the healthy position of experiencing constructive negative emotions (of whatever level of intensity) would be overlooked.

Another group of clients, when asked about their therapeutic goals, state that they want to feel calm or indifferent when facing the activating event about which they are currently anxious. According to REP, such goals are problematic and unrealistic. Let us again take Rex's example to illustrate this point. Again you will recall that Rex's anxiety stems from the following irrational beliefs that he holds about possibly failing his driving test: (1) I must pass my driving test; and (2) If I fail my driving test it will prove I'm an idiot. In order to feel calm or indifferent about the test, Rex would have to believe the following: I don't care whether or not I pass my driving test; it really doesn't matter to me. Now unless Rex is taking the driving test for the sake of someone else (e.g. his father – see above) the fact that he is anxious about the test, in all probability, indicates that beneath his musturbatory belief, there is a healthy rational belief such as (1) I want to pass my driving test, but I don't have to do so;(2) If I fail my driving test, I can still accept myself as a fallible human being. I would not be an idiot. Given the existence of his rational belief, Rex could only become indifferent about the driving test by lying to himself and denying that he actually wanted to pass it, i.e. he has to pretend that he does not have a healthy rational belief. Since people do not overcome their emotional problems in the long term by lying to themselves, a more effective solution is to help them with their problems by encouraging them to change their irrational beliefs to rational beliefs rather than by promoting beliefs of indifference.

People often have mixed emotions

In reading this discussion of emotions, you could be forgiven if you thought that people only experience one emotion at a time. In fact, people often experience a mix of emotions, although one particular emotion might predominate. Let me give another example to demonstrate this point. Anna, a 23-year-old woman, wanted to go to a school reunion on a date that clashed with an arrangement she had already made with her fiancé. When she asked him whether or not he minded if she went, he replied that he did and said that he would feel quite hurt if she decided to go.

Anna had a number of different emotions about this; she felt angry, guilty and anxious. How do we explain this? Rational–emotive psychologists would say that the reason that Anna had different emotions about her fiancé's reaction is twofold: first, she focuses at slightly different times on different aspects of the broad A (activating event) and second, she brings a set of (in this case) irrational beliefs to these three specific, but different A's (see Figure 5.5).

1. Anna's anger
   A: He's putting unfair pressure on me.
   B: He absolutely shouldn't do this to me.
   C: Anger

2. Anna's guilt
   A: I've hurt his feelings.
   B: I absolutely shouldn't have done that.
      I'm selfish and something of a bad person for doing this.
   C: Guilt

3. Anna's anxiety
   A: Prospect of fiancé ending the relationship (if I decide to go to the reunion).
   B: This must not happen.
      I couldn't bear it if he broke our engagement.
   C: Anxiety

Figure 5.5. ABC analysis of Anna's mixed unconstructive negative emotions.

As Figure 5.5 shows, Anna focuses on different aspects of the broad situation. Note that these different aspects are in reality inferences about different features of the broad A. First, when she is angry, Anna focuses on her fiancé's motives and on the fairness (or otherwise) of his behaviour, and she makes the inference 'He's putting unfair pressure on me', which she evaluates irrationally 'He absolutely shouldn't do this to me'.

Second, when she is feeling guilty, Anna focuses on the effect that her wish to attend the reunion has on her fiancé and makes the inference 'I've hurt his feelings', which she again evaluates irrationally 'I absolutely shouldn't have done that'.

Finally, when she is feeling anxious, Anna makes a prediction of what might happen if she goes ahead and attends the reunion, and she infers that her fiancé might end their relationship, which she once again evaluates irrationally 'This must not happen. I couldn't bear it if he broke our engagement'.

Any of these three feelings might predominate at any given moment according to which aspect of the situation Anna focuses on at that time and the inference she makes (with the associated irrational belief) about that aspect. If Anna is particularly preoccupied with any one aspect of this situation, the emotion that stems from her inference and irrational belief about that aspect will be her predominant emotion. Thus, if she is particularly preoccupied with the prospect of her fiancé ending their relationship should she decide to go to the reunion, then because she holds an irrational belief about that inference, her predominant emotion will be anxiety.

The same process would hold true if Anna only held rational beliefs about the three different aspects of the broad situation (see Figure 5.6).

1. Anna's annoyance
   A: He's putting unfair pressure on me.
   B: I'd prefer it if he didn't put unfair pressure on me, but there's no reason why he must not do this.
   C: Annoyance

2. Anna's remorse
   A: I've hurt his feelings.
   B: I wish I had not hurt his feelings, but I'm not selfish or bad for doing this. I'm a fallible human being who has acted in a way that has had unfortunate results.
   C: Remorse

3. Anna's concern
   A: Prospect of fiancé ending the relationship (if I decide to go to the reunion).
   B: I'd much prefer it if this did not occur, but there's no reason why it must not happen. If it did it would be difficult to tolerate, but not unbearable.
   C: Concern

Figure 5.6. ABC analysis of Anna's mixed constructive negative emotions.

As Figure 5.6 again shows, Anna focuses on different aspects of the broad situation and, as described above, makes a number of inferences about these aspects. First, when she is annoyed, Anna focuses on her fiancé's motives and on the fairness (or otherwise) of his behaviour, and again makes the inference 'He's putting unfair pressure on me', which this time she evaluates rationally: 'I'd prefer it if he didn't put unfair pressure on me, but there's no reason why he must not do this.'

Second, when she is feeling remorse, Anna again focuses on the effect that her wish to attend the reunion has had on her fiancé and makes the same inference 'I've hurt his feelings' which this time she evaluates rationally 'I wish I had not hurt his feelings, but I'm not selfish or bad for doing this. I'm a fallible human being who has acted in a way that has had unfortunate results.'

Finally, when she is feeling concerned, Anna again infers that if she attends the reunion, her fiancé might end their relationship, a possibility which she this time evaluates rationally 'I'd much prefer it if this did not occur, but there's no reason why it must not happen. If it did it would be difficult to tolerate, but not unbearable'.

Again any of these three feelings might predominate at any given moment according to which aspect of the situation Anna focuses on at that time and the inference that she makes (with the associated rational belief) about it. Also, if Anna is particularly preoccupied with any one aspect of this situation, the emotion that stems from her inference and rational belief about that aspect will once again be her predominant emotion. Thus, if she is particularly preoccupied with the pressure that she thinks her fiancé is putting on her, then, because she holds a rational belief about that inference, her predominant emotion will be annoyance.

In conclusion, when Anna experiences a set of constructive negative emotions, a set of unconstructive negative emotions or indeed a combination of the two, she will be aware of feeling a mix of these emotions. In order to make sense of this complex experience, she needs to break it down into its component parts using the ABC framework for each of the specific emotions that comprise her total mixed emotional experience.

One useful way of doing this is for Anna to start at C by listing the different emotions that comprise her total emotional experience. When she has done this, she needs to take one emotion at a time and proceed to A. Thus, if the first emotion she takes is anxiety she needs to ask herself 'What was I most anxious about in the situation I was in?' If she just focuses on her feelings of anxiety, she is more likely to find the answer to this question (which in Anna's case was the prospect that her fiancé might end their engagement) than if she allows her other feelings to intrude. It is important to note that A in such cases is likely to be an inference, as it is in this example.

After she has identified the most relevant A (i.e. her critical A), Anna is now in a position to identify her irrational beliefs about this A which account for her anxiety. Once she has done this she can repeat the entire sequence with the next specific unconstructive negative emotion. In this way Anna can bring order to what otherwise can be a confusing experience.

'False' emotions

It is not possible to tell directly with any degree of certainty that a person is experiencing or has experienced an emotion. We judge that a person has had an emotional experience in two ways. First, we do so by making an interpretation of his non–verbal behaviour (particularly from facial and bodily cues). Second, we do so by accepting at face value his verbal report of how he feels. Although it is possible for a person to dissimulate an emotional state by manufacturing non–verbal behaviour consistent with that state, it is difficult to do so convincingly (although some people are excellent at this, Ronald Reagan being a prime example!). Consequently, paying close attention to this channel of communication often reveals the true emotional state of a person, particularly when there is a discrepancy between his verbal report and his non–verbal behaviour.

Why should someone verbally dissimulate an emotional state? Let me deal with this issue by considering the dissimulation of unconstructive negative emotions. People often claim to be more angrily outraged at an injustice, for example, than they actually feel in order to create a favourable impression in the minds of others. Politicians provide a good example of this. They often claim an exaggerated unconstructive negative emotion in order to be perceived as caring by their constituents. This last point is important. I am saying that some unconstructive negative emotions are generally considered to be a positive response to certain very negative activating events. Under these conditions we are likely to claim an experience of such feelings that we do not actually have, for example, to gain approval from others. The second reason why we may claim to have unconstructive negative emotions that we do not, in fact, experience is to ward off criticism and attack from others. Raymond DiGiuseppe (1988) has commented that we often have rules about how we should feel and this is especially the case with anger. Since we hypothesise that we may be viewed negatively if we were to say that we feel only mildly angry about an injustice or even strongly annoyed (but not angry) about it, we verbally exaggerate our feelings so that we are not viewed negatively.

The same process occurs with guilty self–blame. Some years ago, one of my students came to see me in an agitated manner. She had not completed an assignment on time and appeared very guilty about this, overtly blaming herself in a very critical manner. I responded with reassurance urging her not to be so hard on herself. She calmed down to some extent and left after we had discussed some aspects of her work. Ten minutes later, during my walk across campus, I saw this student laughing and joking with some of her friends. I was struck by the contrast between the disturbed state she had been in ten minutes earlier and this happy-go-lucky mood. I mentioned this to a colleague, who had also experienced the sudden shift of mood in this student. Years later I met this student and discussed the incident with her. She admitted that at that time she had used 'turning on the tears' as she called it to ward off criticism and get her out of tricky situations. This forcefully brought home to me the ability of people to manufacture emotion for specific ends. It is these manufactured emotions that I refer to as 'false' emotions.

The manufacturing of 'false' emotions is one strategy that people employ to negotiate their way through life, sometimes attempting to gain something positive and at other times attempting to avoid something negative. I come back to these strategies in the next chapter which considers rational–emotive psychology's perspective on behaviour.

Chapter 6
Behaviour

In the ABC framework that is so central to rational-emotive psychology, C stands for the emotional *and* behavioural consequences of holding evaluative beliefs (B) about A. In the previous chapter, I considered emotional C's and discussed several important issues with respect to the REP view of emotions. I now turn my attention to behavioural C's and consider a number of important issues that emerge when we look at the REP view of behaviour.

Behaviour is purposive

When a person acts in a certain way, that action can be seen as having a purpose, i.e. through that behaviour the person is seeking to achieve something. The person may not be aware of this purpose, but this does not negate the REP proposition that much behaviour is purposive. The main purposes of behaviour are:

I   to initiate an emotional state;
II to stop an emotional state;
III to avoid an emotional state;
IV to reduce the intensity of an emotional state;
V   to intensify an emotional state;
VI to maintain an emotional state;
VII to elicit a response from the physical environment;
VIII to elicit a response from the interpersonal environment; and
IX to act in a way that is consistent with one's values, standards and goals.

I deal with each of these purposes in turn and show when such behaviour stems from irrational beliefs.

Purposive behaviour I: To initiate an emotional state

A person may act to initiate either a positive or a negative emotional state. Let us take the former situation first. When considering the purposes of behaviour, it is important to distinguish between short-term goals and long-term goals. Rational-emotive psychology posits that we are at our happiest when actively pursuing meaningful and absorbing long-term goals. When we act in the service of these long-term goals, we often have to put up with short-term discomfort. We do so because we think that it is worth it and because we are committed to the idea that our present behaviour will bring long-term happiness. In this important sense behaviour can lead to a projected positive emotional state (see also Purpose IX, pp.76–77).

Now let me consider behaviour where the purpose is to initiate shorter-term positive emotional states. We are all familiar with the desire to seek out a positive emotional state when feeling bored, for example. Thus, we may actively involve ourselves in an interest so that we may gain a present sense of enjoyment. Also, we may turn to pleasurable immediate diversions, such as playing a favourite cassette tape or reading a novel. These activities are generally healthy for us unless they also serve a different purpose, e.g. helping us to avoid something that we need to face up to (see pp. 67–68).

Conversely, we may pursue enjoyable experiences which are more dangerous. Thus, we may seek out activities which contain a high element of risk, like pot-holing, rock-climbing and para-gliding. If we are highly skilled in these activities then we will reduce the risk, but for those who seek thrills, the element of risk is what makes the activity thrilling. Alternatively, we may take drugs to initiate a highly pleasurable state. The risks of drug-taking are well known and some drugs are so addictive that we may very quickly take them for a different purpose – to get rid of the highly unpleasant emotional state known as withdrawal. Later in this chapter, I discuss behaviour, the purpose of which is to stop an emotional state. When a person engages in behaviour designed to initiate a short-term intensely pleasurable state, but which places that person's well-being in danger, it may be that he holds the following irrational belief: 'I must experience these pleasurable feelings and I can't stand depriving myself of such feelings when they are so readily available to me.'

Behaviour can also have the purpose of initiating a negative emotional state. This may seem to be a strange idea, but the phenomenon does occur in clinical practice. Richard Wessler and Sheenah Hankin-Wessler, two psychotherapists who work in North America argue that some people behave in a way to provoke a negative feeling in themselves. It is important to stress that this process is not a conscious one. The person does not say to himself: 'I think I will do this because it will lead me to feel bad.' He acts, however, as if this was his motivation. Why should a person act to feel bad? The Wesslers argue that he does so because this negative feeling is familiar to him.

Let me give an example of this phenomenon. Joe, a 27-year-old mature student, has a history of failing courses at college and yet persists at his studies, moving from one subject to another in the hope of succeeding at something. At the time of the incident that I will describe, he was studying drama and was doing very well. It looked as if for the first time in his life Joe would be successful at a college subject. His essay marks were good, his acting skills were first-class; all Joe had to do to achieve his qualification was to hand in a practical log. The long-awaited success was close at hand. Or was it? As you may surmise, Joe found a way to sabotage his success. In this case he developed crippling writer's block. Interestingly, this did not develop until his success was in sight. In therapy, it emerged that although Joe was very uncomfortable with the view that he had about himself, namely that he was a failure, he was also comfortable with this familiar self-view because it enabled him to predict the world with some degree of certitude. The prospect of succeeding, then, led Joe to sabotage his position by developing writer's block. Remember, Joe was not aware of the sabotaging aspect of his behaviour; it occurred outside of his awareness.

As long as there was a chance of passing his course, Joe could not write. His overcame his block only several weeks after it became apparent that once again he had failed. Joe's feelings about yet another failure were mixed. On the one hand and consciously, he was very disappointed to have failed once again. On the other hand, he was secretly relieved that he did not have to confront unfamiliar situations to which his success would have, in his mind, inevitably led. His failure gave him that sense of familiarity that his writer's block was designed to bring about. To put it more graphically, Joe snatched failure from the jaws of success. His behaviour enabled him to feel the familiar, but painful, feelings that were associated with his belief that he was a failure. Of course part of Joe wanted to succeed and this explained why a few months later he enrolled on a different course, destined no doubt to repeat a painful, but familiar script unless he can use his understanding of the dynamics of his situation to bring about a change in his attitude towards himself and thereby stop himself from behaving in a way that initiates a negative emotional state.

As this example shows, behaviour can serve several different purposes simultaneously. Thus, Joe's behaviour was not only designed to initiate a negative emotional state, i.e. feelings of failure, it was simultaneously designed to initiate a sense of familiarity which can be regarded as a positive aspect of his overall emotional state. Note that an emotional experience can have both positive and negative aspects.

Although behaviour is multi-purposive, I will deal in this chapter with one major purpose at a time.

Purposive behaviour II: To terminate an emotional state

We may also behave in ways to rid ourselves of emotional states that are negative and positive. Let me consider the cessation of negative states first. When we are bored we may act to end this emotional state. Here, our primary purpose is to stop the boredom rather than to seek pleasure. Again, it is important to distinguish between unpleasantness-ceasing behaviours that are relatively harmless and those that are self-defeating or downright dangerous. I have already mentioned drug-taking as an example of the latter, so let me briefly discuss behaviours, the purpose of which is to dispose of an unpleasant emotional state, but which turn out to be self-defeating for the individual.

A good example of this is when a person leaves a situation when he is anxious. The purpose of this withdrawal is to end the person's anxiety and in this respect it is frequently successful. However, and this point needs to be underscored, such behaviour often leads to greater problems for the individual in the future. I discuss this more fully in Chapter 8. For now, I want to stress that such withdrawal tends to reinforce the person's irrational beliefs that underpin his anxiety and deprives him of an opportunity of identifying, challenging and eventually changing these beliefs. Let me exemplify these points.

Jim, a 25-year-old insurance clerk tends to get anxious in social situations. Whenever his anxiety level increases beyond a point that he is prepared to tolerate, he leaves the situation, and excuses himself, claiming that he has a headache or some other minor pain. Jim's anxiety is based primarily on the following irrational belief: 'I must not say anything foolish in public. If I do, it would be awful and would prove what a fool I am.' This belief leads him to stay silent much of the time, the purpose of which is to minimise Jim's anxiety – I will discuss this purpose more fully later in this chapter. More importantly, this belief triggers Jim's anxiety when it becomes clear to him that he cannot stay silent any longer. At this point, he withdraws from the situation, the purpose of which is to bring Jim's anxiety to an end. When Jim leaves the social situation he implicitly believes the following: 'Oh my God! People are looking at me and they expect me to say something. I have to get away before I make a fool of myself.' As he leaves at this point, he not only reinforces his irrational belief, but he also deprives himself of opportunities of showing himself (1) that while he would prefer it if he did not say something stupid in public, there is no law of the universe that says that he must not do so, and (2) that he is not a fool for saying something foolish in company, but a fallible human being who has said the wrong thing.

A person can also behave in a way to terminate a positive emotional state. Take the example of Wendy, a 34-year-old woman who is studying hard for her professional accountancy exams. One evening she takes a break from her studies to go out with two college friends. She intends to stay out for only a couple of hours but in fact finds herself spending several hours with them. When she focuses on how much she is enjoying herself, she explains that she has to go home and promptly leaves. What is happening here is that when Wendy realises what a good time she is having, she leaves because she believes that she absolutely should not be enjoying herself at a time when she should be studying. As she believes that she has not earned her enjoyment, she cuts it short.

Purposive behaviour III: To avoid an emotional state

People frequently act in a way so as to avoid an emotional state. Let us first consider an instance of a person avoiding an unpleasant emotional state. A good example of this would be procrastinating behaviours that involve putting tasks off till later. While there are several reasons why people procrastinate, here I will deal with one of the major reasons, i.e. the avoidance of discomfort. I used to work in a university counselling service and during that time I saw many students who came for help with their procrastination. When I asked them why they put off studying, a large number replied that they never seemed to be in the mood. While this by no means fully explains procrastinating behaviour, it is a key dynamic of such behaviour.

According to the present analysis, we can understand procrastination as behaviour whose purpose is partly to help the person avoid experiencing an unpleasant emotional state, in this case discomfort, since these students would have initially felt uncomfortable if they had done something (in this case studying) that they were not in the mood for.

Such avoidance behaviour can come in different guises. First, some students would involve themselves in pleasurable diversions. While on the surface such behaviour seems as if its purpose is to initiate a pleasurable emotional state, and of course there is that element to it, the main goal of such behaviour was to help the people concerned to avoid the experience of discomfort. Second, other students would engage in passive avoidance activities, such as sleeping, day-dreaming and simply sitting for long periods of time in a chair thinking about getting down to work. Third, yet other students became engaged in what I call 'pseudo-work'. Here they would involve themselves in activities that could be mistaken for work, but when considered carefully turn out to be avoidance behaviour. Examples of pseudo-work include arranging one's books in order so that one can get easy access to relevant material, tidying one's desk so that one has plenty of space in which to work and ensuring that one's pens are properly filled with ink and one's pencils are properly sharpened.

You may wonder how to judge whether such activities constitute work or pseudo-work because they appear to be work-related. Indeed, it is difficult to make such a distinction on casual inspection. If we take a closer look, however, certain revealing clues become apparent. First of all, how long is the person taking over the activity? If it is work-related, then it should not take long and the person is not likely to be too precise in how exact the tidying is, for example. However, if it is avoidance pseudo-work, the person takes an inordinately long time over the activity, which he or she carries out with almost obsessive precision. Second, how frequently does the person perform the activity? If it is work-related, then the person carries out the activity once, while if it is pseudo-work the person repeats the activity fairly frequently instead of getting down to the real work. Third, does the completion of the activity lead to real work being done? If it is work-related the person gets down to the real business of studying as soon as the activity has been completed. If it is basically avoidance in nature, however, the completion of the task does not lead to the initiation of the real business of studying. Rather, the student thinks enough has been done for the day and decides to 'finish work', which is a rationalisation. Finally, in his or her heart of hearts, can the person admit to the avoidance nature of these pseudo-work activities. You will note from the above discussion that a person can easily deceive him- or herself that he or she is engaged in real work when in fact what is engaged in is pseudo-work discomfort-avoidance procrastination. If, however, the student can be honest about it, the person often knows deep down whether he or she is actually working or engaged in pseudo-work avoidance.

It follows from all this that part of adopting an anti-procrastination philosophy involves admitting to oneself that one is avoiding discomfort, seeing the long-term futility of doing so and then courting and staying with discomfort until one becomes comfortable doing the task that is worth tackling in the long run.

Purposive behaviour IV: To reduce the intensity of an emotional state

If a person cannot stop an emotional state or take steps to avoid experiencing it, there is still the opportunity of reducing its intensity. This principle applies to both negative and positive emotional states. Let me consider this principle by dealing first with how people tend to minimise negative emotional states.

Georgina is a 45-year-old woman who experiences anxiety and occasional panic attacks while shopping. Prior to seeking professional help for these problems she developed a number of behavioural strategies, the purpose of which was to reduce or minimise her anxiety as best she could. Thus she developed a number of distraction techniques to use when she became anxious.

First, she would she sing nursery rhymes in her head. This is a form of covert behaviour which she used to distract herself from her anxiety and which worked temporarily by reducing her anxiety level.

Second, whenever this method proved unsuccessful, she would read her shopping list, *sotto voce*. This is a form of verbal behaviour which again had the intent and effect of bringing her anxiety within manageable limits, albeit temporarily.

Third, when her anxiety began to spiral into panic, she used more overt forms of behaviour to bring her feelings under some sort of control. If she was shopping with her husband or with a friend, she would grip tightly the other person's arm so that she did not faint – dizziness and the inference that one will faint is a common symptom of intense anxiety or panic. When her panic grew in intensity, Georgina would grip her shopping trolley so hard that her knuckles would turn white. At the peak of her panic, when she thought that she was beginning to have a heart attack – again a not uncommon inference in panic states – Georgina would stop walking and rest against a supporting wall until her feelings of panic reduced in intensity and became barely manageable anxiety.

At this point, Georgina would get the person accompanying her to queue up to pay for the shopping while she left the supermarket, an overt behavioural strategy which was designed to eliminate her negative feelings and which invariably had that effect. On the rare occasion when she went shopping on her own, Georgina would abandon her shopping trolley in an aisle and run out of the supermarket, which again served to rid herself of her panicky feelings.

The above pattern of covert, verbal and overt behaviours, all designed to reduce the intensity of anxious and panicky feelings, is typical of those who suffer from panic attacks.

We can also use a number of behavioural strategies to reduce the intensity of positive emotional states although, as you can appreciate, we employ these less frequently than we use strategies to reduce the intensity of negative states. Why would we want to reduce the intensity of positive emotional states? First, we may do so because we believe that we do not deserve to be so happy or to experience so much pleasure. We may think this either because we consider that we have not done anything to merit such happiness or pleasure or because it is not right for us to be so happy when others whom we know are unhappy. These two views are frequently expressions of an irrational belief: I must not retain advantages when I have not done anything to deserve them or when others whom I care about are disadvantaged.

A second reason why we may act to reduce the intensity of positive emotional states is because we fear that something very bad may happen if we are that happy. I call this the 'evil eye' belief. Here we believe that we must not feel so good because if we do we will be penalised or even punished for our good fortune. This is particularly the case when we consider that we have not done anything to merit such happiness or pleasure. If we do we are tempting fate and we must act to reduce the intensity of our happiness before the evil eye, or some deity or spirit, spies our good fortune and brings misfortune on our heads to 'even up the score'.

A third reason why we may act to reduce the intensity of our positive feelings is because we fear that we may lose control if we do not. Here our irrational belief is likely to be: 'I must not lose control because if I do terrible things may happen'.

This belief and the pleasure-reducing activities that leads to them often occur in the area of sex, particularly orgasm. For example, Fiona, a 27-year-old woman, sought counselling for anorgasmia (failure to achieve orgasm during intercourse). It transpired that she felt 'unable to let go' during intercourse with her husband. Whenever she began to feel a certain degree of pleasure she would distract herself either by thinking neutral thoughts or by changing her physical position to reduce the intensity of her positive feelings. Fiona was helped through counselling to overcome this problem by first learning to experience orgasm through masturbation (which she had never practised). She learned here that she could experience orgasm without losing total control of herself and then was able to transfer this insight to love-making with her husband.

Purposive behaviour V: To intensify an emotional state

People have been taking steps to intensify their positive emotional states since time immemorial. The desire to experience more pleasure and to feel happier has motivated people to experiment with unusual and, in some cases, highly dangerous behavioural practices. When due care and attention is taken during attempts to intensify positive emotional states and there are no long-term negative effects of such behaviour, then there is usually no problem. Indeed, some highly erotic, safe sexual practices have emerged from people's quest to increase their pleasure.

Quite frequently, however, and especially when a person holds an irrational belief about intensification of pleasure, for example: 'I must increase the low or moderate level of pleasure that I feel and damn the consequences', he or she is likely to engage in behaviour that is more dangerous and self-defeating. The following is a tragic example of the dangers of seeking to intensify one's positive emotional state in a demanding, musturbatory manner.

Recently, in Britain, an MP was found dead in his flat. It was believed that he died from asphyxiation as a result of engaging in a sexual practice known as auto-erotic asphyxia. This term describes the practice, mainly engaged in by men, whereby a man strives to intensify his experience of orgasm by cutting off temporarily the supply of oxygen to his brain. This is accomplished by such methods as tying a ligature tightly around one's neck or placing a plastic bag over one's head. As you can tell from my description, this is a highly dangerous practice which, in Britain, counts for around 200 deaths a year.

So far I have referred to ways in which people may intensify their physical pleasure without recourse to mood-altering drugs. Now I briefly discuss the many ways in which we use artificial means to amplify our pleasure. People have been using substances to intensify their positive experiences throughout history. These substances vary from the slightly unhealthy to the highly toxic and addictive. It is important here to distinguish between what effect the person expects the substance to induce and the substance's actual effect. Thus, someone may take LSD wishing to intensify his or her positive mood, but the actual effect may be very different – he or she may have a 'bad trip'. From the present analysis it is the person's expectations which guide his or her behaviour.

It is not only in the realm of physical pleasure that we strive to intensify our positive emotional states. We also act to intensify our sense of meaning and purpose. Thus, we may develop a growing interest in a project and choose to deepen that interest, and the sense of personal meaning that accompanies it, through behaviours which increase our active involvement in that project. These may include information-seeking activities, actively involving ourselves with others who share our interests, and carrying out new mini-projects to add to our own, and other people's, knowledge and interest.

Less frequently, people may act to intensify a negative emotional state. This happens particularly with guilt. Let me give an example. Bernice, a 37-year-old woman has successfully kept to a weight-reducing diet for a week. Then, at a social gathering she eats more than her diet allows. She feels guilty about this because she believes that she is 'a greedy pig who absolutely shouldn't have let myself go like that'. When she arrives home, still feeling very guilty, she opens the door of the refrigerator and embarks on a huge eating 'binge'. Predictably she intensifies her guilt. It is important to note that Bernice's 'binging' behaviour could have had several different purposes. For example, she may have embarked on a binge to terminate her feelings of guilt, however temporarily. Yet, she considered it an example of guilt intensifying behaviour. This is what she said later:

When I got home from the party, I really felt bad, really guilty. I'd done so well on the diet and then in a matter of hours I felt that I had blown it. I remember thinking when I get home, 'Right now I'm going to do something to really feel guilty about.' So I went on an enormous binge. That did the trick!

Purposive behaviour VI: To maintain an emotional state

After a morning swim at the local swimming pool, I like to have a long hot shower. I notice that I have developed a number of washing rituals, the purpose of which, I have discovered, is to lengthen the time I spend in the shower. Why do I spend so long in the shower? It is not to ensure that I am perfectly clean! Rather it is to maintain, for as long as possible, the pleasurable feelings I get from being under the hot, steamy water.

The points that I made with respect to behaviour, which is designed to initiate or intensify positive emotional states, are also relevant to behaviour, the purpose of which is to maintain such a state. Such behaviour is problematic (1) if it stems from an irrational belief – in which case the person is likely to maintain the positive state for longer than is healthy for him; (2) if it is intrinsically unhealthy for the individual, e.g. if it involves the use of drugs; and (3) if it interferes with the person's healthy goals. Otherwise, there is probably nothing wrong with behaviour, the purpose of which is to maintain our positive feelings.

An example of behaviour whose purpose is to maintain a negative emotional state is procrastination, which is designed to keep the person in a chronic negative state known as a rut, and which also serves to stop the person from experiencing more acute negative feelings. The person puts off doing anything which might result in getting out of the rut because from this perspective it appears that there are only two choices: either he or she feels anxious if he or she were to move out of this rut (because the person holds an irrational belief about change); or he or she feels a comfortable, but negative, sense of lack of fulfilment. Faced with such a choice, it is understandable why someone would act to maintain a negative rut.

Of course the person does have other options. For example, it is possible to do something to identify, challenge and change the irrational beliefs that underpin this acute fear of change. In the absence of other perceived options, however, the person will often act to perpetuate this rut. Thus, when faced with the prospect of gaining promotion, the person might find him- or herself forgetting to hand in the application on time, or not doing well at the promotion interview. As I have mentioned before, such behaviour is not deliberate in the sense that the person says consciously to himself, 'Quick, I need to find some way of remaining in my rut. I know, I will forget to hand my application form in.' Nevertheless, the person acts as if this is what he or she believes.

Purposive behaviour VII: To elicit a response from the physical environment

Imagine that you have a bank card which you can use in a wall cash dispenser machine. You insert the card into the appropriate aperture and follow a number of simple instructions which are flashed up on the machine's screen. Why do you do this? Simply because you want cash and you have learned that if you follow a number of steps you will receive the amount you requested. This is an everyday example of behaviour the purpose of which is to elicit an immediate response from the physical environment. If you fail to receive your cash on a number of occasions when you insert your card you will at some point refrain from carrying out this behavioural sequence.

Similar principles operate when behaviour is designed to elicit a long-term response from the physical environment. If you are a farmer, you are prepared to put in a great deal of effort to plant seeds on the assumption that this effort will yield a crop of produce much later in the year. If this outcome does not occur in response to a small number of planting attempts, you will be loathe to continue your planting behaviour unless you can identify what has gone wrong and can take remedial steps.

Thus, if your behaviour is designed to elicit an immediate or long-term response from the physical environment, you are likely to continue your behaviour if it produces that response and to discontinue your behaviour if it does not produce the response. At what point you will decide to discontinue depends on a number of complex factors which will vary from situation to situation. However, one important variable concerns a person's beliefs. Thus, if a person holds an irrational belief, he or she is more likely to persist with unsuccessful goal-directed behaviour than if that person thinks rationally. The reasons for this persistence are twofold. First, if the person believes that he or she must get what he or she wants from the physical environment, then the person is more likely to keep striving for the goal when it is objectively clear that it cannot be achieved than if he or she holds a comparable rational belief: 'I want to get what I want, but I don't have to get it.' The rigid demand will interfere with the ability to see clearly that the goal is not achievable while his or her flexible preference will aid objectivity. Second, this person's rigid insistence that what he or she wants must be obtained from the physical environment will interfere with the ability to identify and experiment with alternative behaviours, one of which may help to achieve the goal. By contrast, the person's flexible preference will encourage him or her to stand back and consider other behavioural options.

If your behaviour is sometimes rewarded with the intended response and sometimes not, you will continue this behaviour far longer than if your behaviour consistently goes unrewarded. This principle of intermittent reinforcement of behaviour leading to the persistence of that behaviour is the rule that accounts for the maintenance of gambling, for example. Again, you will be more likely to persist with intermittently reinforced behaviour if you think irrationally about your goal than if you think rationally about it.

Purposive behaviour VIII: To elicit a response from the interpersonal environment

We frequently act to elicit a response from other people. Again, as mentioned earlier, it is important to distinguish between a behaviour's purpose and its effect, because in the interpersonal arena we may well elicit the opposite response from people other than we intend. Let me give an example of such behaviour.

Interpersonal purposes of sulking

A number of years ago I published the first ever book written on sulking, which was entitled *The Incredible Sulk* (Dryden, 1992). Before I wrote that book, I (together with my research assistant, Caroline Dearden) interviewed a number of women on their experiences of sulking – we could not find any men who would admit to sulking! As part of that research, I looked at the purposive aspects of sulking. In considering the types of interpersonal responses that people who sulk hope to elicit from others (see Figure 6.1), I will use the actual words of the women we interviewed to illustrate my points. Bear in mind when considering these interpersonal purposes of sulking that sulking itself stems from a set of irrational beliefs about certain activating events at A. If the person thought more rationally about these events he or she would not sulk. Rather they would assert themselves constructively with the other person concerned – behaviour which would seek a different, healthier set of responses from the other. See "The Incredible Sulk" for a fuller discussion of this issue.

1. To punish the other person

Here the person wants to elicit a 'feeling' response in another, but in a way that avoids head-on confrontation. As Rosita noted, 'Sulking is a weapon to show that I have been upset and to retaliate without an actual confrontation ... to make that person feel bad.'

1. To punish the other person
2. To get what I want
3. To get the other person to make the first move
4. To extract proof of caring from the other person

Figure 6.1. Interpersonal purposes of sulking

2. To get what I want

Here the person finds that sulking works because it achieves what he or she wants. Jackie offers her opinion that 'because men in general are pretty insensitive, usually in order to make your point you have to impinge upon their lives and make them uncomfortable'. Jackie has discovered that sulking works for her because it impinges on her husband and makes him uncomfortable. As Jackie says, 'I regard sulking as a means to an end ... to get what I want ... Sulking really can be quite a powerful weapon ... I am not giving it up.'

3. Getting the other person to make the first move

As I said in *The Incredible Sulk*:

> Getting the other to make the first move is frequently based on the unconstructive idea:
> 'I must be treated fairly and since you have treated me unfairly, it's awful. Poor me!' The resulting feeling of hurt then leads to the attitude 'You must make the first move to make me feel better.' In order for this purpose to work, we have to remain in reasonable proximity with the other to be available to receive his or her first move (Dryden, 1992, p. 39).

Mary illustrates this purpose quite well: 'If I sulk it's because I'm hurt and I want someone to come to me. I want the attention brought to me. I want someone to come to me and say "I'm sorry, I didn't mean it." I want them to come to me and apologise to me, so it's manipulative.'

4. To extract proof of caring from the other person

This purpose differs from the one described above because, in example 3, the person sulks to get an apology from the other person, whereas here the person sulks to elicit caring from the other. Sometimes the other person is made to work quite hard in this respect. As Pamela says, 'When I sulk, I really make it difficult for John to find out what's wrong. If he persists long enough, and sometimes it's a very long time, I know that he loves me and then I'll tell him what's wrong.'

As these examples show once again, a single piece of behaviour can have quite different interpersonal purposes. It follows then that if you want to identify the interpersonal purpose of behaviour such as sulking it is important to do so from the perspective of the person responsible for the behaviour. It would be easy, for example, to view sulking simply as a manipulative ploy to get the person what he or she wants. However, as the examples in this section show, this is not the case.

Purposive behaviour IX: To act in a way that is consistent with one's values, standards and long-term goals

I was once told an interesting story to demonstrate that people can act in accordance with their own behavioural standards and not just in response to the behaviour of others. Two businessmen travelled to work everyday by train. When they reached their destination, one of the men was in the habit of buying a daily newspaper from a nearby newspaper vendor. Everyday the vendor growled at the man and everyday the man was very polite in response. This happened every working day for 2 years before the other man enquired of his colleague: 'Why are you so polite to the newspaper vendor when he is so rude to you?' The other man replied: 'Because I choose to act according to my standard of politeness rather than according to his standard of rudeness.'

This example nicely demonstrates the point that I wish to make here: that a person's behaviour can have the purpose of actualising his or her values, standards and long-term goals. To do this, the person does have to think rationally. Thus, the man in the above example probably holds the following rational belief: 'I don't have to respond to the newspaper vendor in the manner in which he treats me.'

A friend of mine once worked in an organisation where pilfering of office supplies was rife. My friend, however, not only refused to take even a single paper clip, he reported the pilfering of his work colleagues to the head of the organisation who instituted an enquiry into the whole affair. My friend did this even though he guessed that he would be shunned by his colleagues as a result. This was, in fact, what happened and my friend spent a very uncomfortable 6 months in a hostile work environment before he left the company for another job. My friend admitted that it would have been very easy for him to keep quiet about the pilfering, but he said that doing so would have gone against his moral values of honesty and good citizenship. He chose to act in a way that was consistent with his values, even though doing so led to a great deal of personal discomfort. He was able to do this because he had a rational belief about receiving disapproval from others and about being uncomfortable.

Finally, let me consider that behaviour which is used to help the individual pursue his or her long-term goals. Rational-emotive psychology considers that it is a mark of positive mental health for a person to pursue long-term goals while tolerating the short-term discomfort of doing so.

About a year ago, I decided to embark on an exercise regimen whereby I would jog or swim 20 minutes a day, 5 days a week. I decided on this programme in order to maintain my health. Everyday, when I wake up, I do not want to go out to exercise and yet I go. I do so first because I choose to behave in a way that is consistent with my long-term health goals and is inconsistent with my short-term comfort goals, and second, because I have a rational belief about short-term discomfort.

In the following two sections of this chapter, I discuss two concepts that are important in understanding rational-emotive psychology's view of behaviour: action tendencies and response options. In doing so, I concentrate on situations where the person is experiencing an unconstructive negative emotion.

Action tendencies

Whenever a person experiences an emotion, he has a tendency to act in a broad manner. As we see in Chapter 7, different emotions lead to different action tendencies. In the previous section, I made the point that much behaviour is purposive and certainly when we tend to act in certain ways depending on the emotion we are experiencing, our resulting behaviour is purposive. Under these circumstances our specific behaviour serves to help us achieve a particular goal. However, these goals or purposes which shape our behaviour are influenced to a large extent by the emotions that we experience. Thus action tendencies are in large part determined by emotions.

As I illustrate in the following chapter, when a person experiences unconstructive negative emotions, the goals are likely to be self-protective in the short-term – they influence the person to act in ways that reduce or terminate these emotions – but self-defeating in the longer term – they do not help the person to face up to and deal constructively with negative A's. When that person experiences constructive negative emotions, however, his or her goals are more likely to be self-enhancing in both the short- and the long-term, because that person will be less likely to strive to reduce or terminate these emotions and will be more likely to deal constructively with the negative events at A.

Action tendencies are general categories of behaviour rather than specific pieces of behaviour. Moreover, different specific behaviours can actualise a given action tendency. For example, as I discuss in the next chapter, a major action tendency that flows from the emotion of anger urges us to attack the person about whom we are angry. There are a number of ways, however, in which we can carry out such an attack: directly, either physically or verbally; or indirectly, such as attacking the person's reputation by spreading rumours behind his or her back, or by destroying a valued possession without him or her knowing who perpetrated such an attack. Each of these different specific behaviours are concrete expressions of the same, much broader action tendency.

Response options

Response options are behavioural possibilities that exist in a given situation. Such options might include ways of acting which serve:

1. To actualise the action tendency;
2. To go against the action tendency in a way that is constructive; and
3. To compensate the person influenced by the action tendency.

Additionally, one can choose ways of acting that are not related to the action tendency.

Furthermore, response options that actualise some of the other purposes of behaviour listed on p.63 and discussed earlier in this chapter are also relevant in this context. Let me illustrate, however, two of the types of response options listed above by continuing with the example of anger and the associated action tendency of attack. I have already shown that we can attack another person with whom we are angry by choosing among a number of specific attack-related response options, so let me begin by discussing constructive response options that go against this action tendency.

Constructive response options that go against an action tendency

A constructive alternative to attacking another person is to assert ourselves with him or her. However, in order to do this effectively, we need to hold rational rather than irrational beliefs. While it is possible for us to assert ourselves constructively with another person when we are angry, such assertive behaviour is likely to break down if that other person does not respond in a likewise constructive manner.

Thus, if we are to utilise a constructive response option that goes against an action tendency that is based on an unhealthy negative emotion (in this case, anger), we first need to challenge and change the irrational beliefs that underpin such an emotion. If we do this, we will experience a healthy negative emotion (in this case, annoyance) and will be influenced by a different action tendency that stems from this emotion (in this case, to deal effectively with the A that we were previously angry about). If we do this, we are likely to sustain assertive behaviour because this response option is now consistent with our new action tendency.

Response options that compensate the person influenced by an action tendency

When we choose a response option that allows us to compensate for an unhealthy negative emotion such as anger, we are still influenced by this emotion, but are able to refrain from actualising the attack action tendency. For example, when we are angry at another person, we may choose to be exceptionally nice to that person. In this case, our nice behaviour enables us to compensate for our anger.

Such compensatory behaviour serves a number of purposes. First, it may help us to avoid experiencing unacceptable emotions. Thus, many people believe that it is wrong to be angry and that they must not experience such an emotion. Being nice to the person with whom we feel an underlying anger, allows us to remain unaware that we are experiencing this forbidden feeling. Second, it may protect us from getting into unwanted trouble with the person with whom we are angry. If we are angry with someone who has power and influence over us then it might not be wise for us to express our anger to that person. So, because we are angry, we compensate by being extra nice to the other person. The same principle applies when we believe that we need the approval of the person with whom we are angry. If we were to attack the person, we would be scared that he or she would disapprove of us, so, again, we compensate for our anger by being overly nice to that person.

The reason why we act especially nicely to the other person under these conditions is that we think that our anger would show if we were to act in an everyday manner with him. Our extra nice behaviour serves to disguise our anger from the other person so that (1) he or she cannot use any power against us, or (2) he or she does not disapprove of us. If we were annoyed rather than angry, however, we would be less likely to resort to the use of this compensatory mechanism because we would be more in control of our feelings and we would be more likely to assert ourselves in a way that does not alienate the other person.

Behavioural competence

Rational-emotive psychology recognises that people may or may not have certain responses in their behavioural repertoire, and it also acknowledges that when these behaviours are in their repertoire, they perform them at varying levels of skill. If a person does not possess such a skill in his or her behavioural repertoire, REP notes that this situation may have arisen as a result of that person holding irrational beliefs. Thus, if you believe that you must do well in conversing with members of the opposite sex, you may well avoid speaking to them; because you avoid doing so, you deprive yourself of valuable opportunities for developing your social skills in this area of your life.

However, it is important for rational-emotive psychologists to avoid taking an inflexible line and assuming that skill deficits always stem from irrational beliefs. They can do, but there are a number of other factors that explain why a person has not developed certain behavioural skills. These include lack of opportunity, exposure to poor role models, lack of aptitude and lack of positive reinforcement for skilled performance. It can be the case that a person may develop irrational beliefs as a result of failing to acquire certain skills and, as I have just described, failure to develop skills may stem from the person holding irrational beliefs. The situation here is 'both/and' rather than 'either/or'. This both/and explanation is also relevant when we account for variations in skill level among people.

Rational-emotive psychologists also consider the inferences and evaluative beliefs that people construct about their level of behavioural competence. For example, at the inferential level, people can either underestimate or overestimate their level of skill or give an improvement in skill level a particular inferential meaning (e.g. 'Now that I can converse more skilfully with women, I will soon lose my virginity'). At the level of evaluative beliefs, people may rate themselves for having a certain level of skill (e.g. 'I'm not as socially skilled as I absolutely should be and as a result I'm no good' – irrational belief) or may evaluate the effort that it may take to become more skilful (e.g. 'It will take a lot of practice to learn more productive study skills. I wish it were easier, but it doesn't have to be any easier than it is. I can tolerate the effort involved' – rational belief).

In this chapter, I have considered the purposive nature of behaviour, the concepts of action tendencies and response options, and the issue of behavioural competence. Having now looked at rational-emotive psychology's stance on activating events, inferences, beliefs, emotions and behaviour, in the following chapter I put this all together and deal with the ABC's of common emotional problems that people experience in their lives.

Chapter 7
Common emotional problems

In this chapter, I consider the common emotional problems that people experience in their lives and that sometimes provide an impetus for them to seek professional help. Thus, I deal with the following emotions: anxiety, depression, anger, guilt, shame, hurt, jealousy and envy. In doing so, I limit my discussion to situations where the person has an emotional problem about something specific in his or her life, whether actual or inferred.

According to rational-emotive psychology, the emotions I have just listed are unconstructive negative emotions (see Chapter 5), because they stem from irrational beliefs and consequently tend to prevent the person from dealing constructively with negative A's that can be changed, or from reconciling himself to negative A's that cannot be changed in a way that permits that subject to get on with his or her life. For each unconstructive negative emotion I discuss the major inferences that people tend to make, the major irrational beliefs that they tend to hold, the cognitive consequences of the emotion and the major action tendencies that flow naturally from the emotion.

After I have considered each unconstructive negative emotion, I discuss the alternative constructive negative emotion. Likewise, I discuss the major inferences, irrational beliefs, cognitive sequelae and action tendencies that go along with each constructive negative emotion. Finally, I discuss meta-emotions, which are the emotions that we feel at C about prior experienced emotions and which then come to serve as A's.

Anxiety

I consider anxiety to be an unconstructive negative emotion, with concern being its constructive negative counterpart.

Inferences

When a person is anxious, he or she has made an inference that a threat exists to his or her personal domain (see Chapter 4). This threat can refer to a future event or to the future implications of a presently occurring event. As I noted in Chapter 3, inferences are hunches about reality that need to be checked out against that reality (as far as this can be done). When a person is anxious, however, he or she assumes that the threat is real and this constitutes the A in the ABC formulation of his or her experience. Of course, A can also refer to an actual threat.

Albert Ellis (1979, 1980), the founder of rational-emotive psychology, argues that, when anxious, a person can infer that there exists a threat either to self worth (this form of anxiety is known as *ego anxiety*) or to the level of personal comfort (known as *discomfort anxiety*). These two forms of anxiety often interact, leading to the spiralling effect of mounting anxiety or panic (see Chapter 8).

Irrational beliefs

The rational-emotive psychology view of anxiety is that it is based on the person's irrational beliefs about the actual or inferred threat. In other words, the person believes a version of one or more of the following beliefs:

1. This threat must not occur.
2. It would be awful if this threat were to occur.
3. I could not bear it if this threat were to occur.
   and in ego anxiety:
4. If this threat were to occur, it would prove that I would be worthless.

Cognitive consequences of anxiety

Once the person brings one or more of these irrational beliefs to the actual or inferred threat, in addition to creating the emotion of anxiety, he or she will have a tendency to think in one or more of the following ways:

1. He or she may overestimate the negative features of the threat;
2. He or she may underestimate her ability to cope within the threat; or
3. He or she may create an even more negative threat in her mind.
4. He or she has more task – irrelevant thoughts than in concern.

Action tendencies and response options

When a person is anxious the major action tendencies are as follows:

1. To withdraw physically from the threat (i.e. by leaving the situation).

2. To withdraw mentally from the threat (e.g. by using distraction techniques).
3. To ward off the threat (e.g. by the use of obsessive compulsive or superstitious behaviour).
4. To tranquillise one's feelings (e.g. by the use of alcohol, legal and illegal drugs, food, cigarettes, etc.).
5. To seek reassurance so that the threat is neutralised in his or her mind.

If actualised, these action tendencies allow the person to terminate any anxiety. In addition, the person may avoid the threat before he or she gets anxious. Avoidance is quite a common action tendency in anxiety. The person avoids the threatening situation because he or she knows, at some level of awareness, that there would be a feeling of anxiety if he or she did not carry out avoidance behaviour.

If the person translates these action tendencies into actual behaviour, then he or she manages to gain short-term relief from anxiety, but unwittingly strengthens those anxiety-creating irrational beliefs. For every time he or she avoids or withdraws from the threat at A, an irrational belief is reinforced: 'I really had to avoid or escape from the threat. It would have been terrible if the threat had materialised and I had to face it.'

As mentioned above, when the person is anxious, he or she considers that it is impossible to deal with the threat if it occurred. Either he or she cannot see clearly that there are more constructive response options (since anxiety tends to interfere with the ability to think clearly), or the person is of the opinion that he or she is unable to execute such responses successfully. This situation tends to add to the person's sense of being overwhelmed by the threat if he or she did not avoid it or withdraw from it quickly.

Concern: the healthy alternative to anxiety

According to rational-emotive psychology, concern is the healthy alternative to anxiety. When a person is feeling concerned, he or she is facing an actual threat or again makes the inference that there is a threat to the personal domain (either to self-worth or to a sense of comfort). However, the following rational beliefs about this threat are held:

1. I would prefer it if this threat did not occur, but there is no reason why it must not happen.
2. It would be bad if this threat occurred, but it would not be terrible.
3. If this threat occurred, it would be difficult to tolerate, but I could bear it.

and in ego anxiety:

4. I would be a fallible human being if this threat were to occur. It would not prove that I am worthless.

When the person is concerned, but not anxious about the threat, he or she: tends not to overestimate the negative features of the threat; does not underestimate his or her ability to cope with the threat; does not create an even more negative threat in his or her mind; and has more task relevant thoughts than in anxiety.

The action tendencies associated with concern are those which encourage the person to face up to the threat and deal with it constructively. Thus, when the person is concerned, he or she is able to identify and select constructive behaviour from the response options.

Depression

Here I consider depression (in its non-clinical sense) to be an unconstructive negative emotion, with sadness being its constructive negative counterpart.

Inferences

When a person is depressed, he or she has experienced a loss, or has made an inference that a loss has occurred from his or her personal domain. This loss can refer, for example, to a loss of a loved one through death or rejection, a loss of a valued possession, a loss of a job or a psychological loss, such as a failure or the loss of an ambition. When the loss is inferential, the inference again needs to be checked out against reality (as far as this can be done). When a person is depressed, however, he or she assumes that the loss has occurred and this constitutes the A in the ABC formulation of his or her experience. As noted in Chapter 3, A can also be an actual loss.

Irrational beliefs

The rational-emotive psychology view of depression is that it is based on the person's irrational beliefs about the actual or inferred loss. Using the definitions of Ellis, we can distinguish between *ego depression*, where the loss triggers ego-related irrational beliefs, and *discomfort depression*, where the loss triggers discomfort-related irrational beliefs. When a person is depressed, then, he or she believes a version of one or more of the following beliefs:

1. My loss absolutely should not have occurred.
2. It is terrible that I have incurred this loss.
3. I cannot tolerate this loss.

and in ego depression:

4. This loss proves that I am worthless.

Paul Hauck (1971), a rational-emotive psychologist, has discussed two types of depression (his third type, self-pity, will be discussed in the section on hurt – see below). First, Hauck (1971) argues, as mentioned above, that depression can occur when the person has a negative view of him- or herself (e.g. 'I am unworthy because I did not do as well on the test as I absolutely should have done'). This is ego depression. Second, depression is related to other-pity. Here, the person focuses on the losses or misfortunes of others and believes: 'Such losses or misfortunes absolutely should not have occurred. The world is a rotten place for allowing such things to happen. Poor them!'

Cognitive consequences of depression

Once the person brings one or more of these irrational beliefs to the actual or inferred loss, in addition to creating depressed feelings, he or she will have a tendency to think in one or more of the following ways:

1. The person may see only the negative aspects of the loss and fail to see any positive features.
2. The person may think of other losses and negative events that he or she has experienced in his or her life.
3. The person may consider that he or she is unable to help him- or herself ('helplessness').
4. The person may see only pain and blackness in the future ('hopelessness').

Action tendencies and response options

When a person is depressed, the major action tendencies are as follows:

1. To withdraw from experiences that were previously reinforcing and from people who were previously valued.
2. To withdraw 'into oneself' and become inactive and inert.
3. To create an environment consistent with the depressed state, e.g. by sitting in the dark, listening to Leonard Cohen albums.
4. To terminate the feelings of depression, e.g. by drinking (this is particularly the case when the person's depressed feelings are not yet severe).

Again if these action tendencies are actualised, the person tends to strengthen the irrational beliefs. Thus, while listening to one of Leonard Cohen's gloomy dirges, the person when depressed can easily conclude: 'He's right. The world really is a rotten place.' Also, with respect to response options, because the person may well be thinking thoughts that are helpless and hopeless, the tendency would be not to do anything constructive to help him- or herself (because the person thinks that he or she is unable to do so and that nothing he or she can do will improve the lot).

Sadness: the healthy alternative to depression

According to rational-emotive psychology, sadness is the healthy alternative to depression. When a person is feeling sad about an actual or inferred loss from the personal domain as it pertains either to self-worth or a sense of comfort, he or she holds the following rational beliefs about this loss:

1. I would prefer it if this loss did not happen, but there is no reason why it must not have occurred.
2. It is bad that I experienced this loss, but it is not terrible.
3. It is difficult to tolerate my loss, but I can bear it.

and in ego depression:

4. Even though I have experienced this loss, I am still a fallible human being and not any less worthy.

Returning to Paul Hauck's (1971) analysis of depression (see p.85), the healthy alternatives to self-downing and other-pity are self-acceptance (see above) and sadness for the plight of others respectively. In the latter, the person focuses on the losses or misfortunes of others and believes: 'It would be very nice if such losses or misfortunes did not happen, but there is no reason, most regrettably, that they absolutely should not have occurred. The world is not a rotten place for allowing such things to happen. It is a mixture of good, bad and neutral features. The people who experienced such losses or misfortunes are not poor creatures to be pitied. They are people in a poor situation to be empathised with and, if possible, helped or encouraged to help themselves.'

When the person is sad, but not depressed about a loss, he or she

1. will more likely be able to see both negative and positive aspects of the loss than when depressed;
2. is less likely to think of other losses and negative events that he or she has experienced in his or her life than when depressed (or, if he or she does think of such events, there is a greater likelihood to see them in the overall perspective of his or her life rather than as part of a mass of negative experiences as when he or she is depressed);
3. is more likely to consider that he or she is able to help him- or

herself than when he or she is depressed ('resourcefulness'); and
4. is able to look into the future with hope.

With respect to action tendencies and response options in sadness, when a person is sad but not depressed about a loss from the personal domain, he or she thinks that it is possible to choose and successfully engage in constructive actions from among the response options. The person is able to actualise the action tendency to express feelings about the loss, and to talk about it with significant others rather than withdraw into him- or herself.

Anger

Here I consider anger to be an unconstructive negative emotion, with annoyance being its constructive negative counterpart. However, some rational-emotive psychologists distinguish between demanding anger (unconstructive negative emotion) and non-demanding anger (constructive negative emotion).

Inferences

When a person is angry, he or she could be making one of a number of inferences. I will deal with three such common inferences, which refer to anger about another person (or persons), and refer the interested reader to Dryden's book on anger for a fuller discussion on this topic (Dryden, 1990).

Frustration

First, when angry, the person, for example a man, could infer that another person (or group of people) has blocked him from achieving something deemed important within his personal domain. This frustration could constitute an impediment to immediate comfort (e.g. someone taking too long to cross a zebra crossing so holding up a car driver) or a block to an important long-term goal (e.g. someone makes his own case for promotion at work to the detriment of the person's desired advancement).

Transgression of a personal rule

Second, when angry, the man could infer that another person (or group of people) has broken one (or more) of his personal rules, which have an important place in the personal domain. These rules constitute the man's views of how other people should (preferably or ideally) behave.

It can happen, of course, that, when this person is angry at someone for transgressing one of his personal rules, this also constitutes a frustration. I prefer, however, to keep the two types of inference separate since the person can anger himself when another breaks his personal rule and he is not personally disadvantaged in any way. Thus, this angering oneself can occur when the person sees someone jumping a queue, even though he or she is not standing in that queue.

Threat to self-esteem

Third, when the person is angry he could be making the inference that the other person's behaviour (or lack of behaviour) constitutes a threat to his self-esteem. It is important to note that this inference is frequently below (or even well below) the person's level of awareness. If asked what he is angry about, the man often provides responses that indicate that he has been making inferences about being frustrated, or that the other person has transgressed an important personal rule. If encouraged, however, to pin-point what he is most angry about or if asked to explore his chain of inferences (as Hawkeye did with B.J. in the example provided in Chapter 3), then the man may well reveal an inference concerning a threat being made to his self-esteem. You may remember that inferring a threat to one's self-esteem is a major inference in anxiety (see pp. 82). Such a threat, however, normally has not yet occurred when the person is anxious, whereas normally it has occurred when the person is angry.

Irrational beliefs

The rational-emotive psychology view of anger is that it is based on the person's irrational beliefs about actual or inferred frustration, other(s) transgressing personal rules or posing a threat to self-esteem. As with anxiety and depression, it is possible to distinguish between *ego anger*, where a threat to self-esteem triggers ego-related irrational beliefs, and *discomfort anger*, where a frustration or rule-transgression triggers discomfort-related irrational beliefs. When a person is angry about being frustrated by another person, for example, he or she believes a version of one or more of the following beliefs:

1. You absolutely should not have frustrated me.
2. It is terrible that you frustrated me.
3. I cannot tolerate being frustrated by you.
4. You are a rotten person for frustrating me

and in ego anger, when the person's self-esteem is threatened by another person:

Common emotional problems

4. You absolutely should not remind me what a worthless person I am.

Cognitive consequences of anger

Once the person brings one or more of these irrational beliefs to the actual or inferred frustration, rule-transgression or threat to self-esteem, in addition to creating angry feelings, he or she will have a tendency to think in one or more of the following ways: he or she may

1. overestimate the extent to which the other person deliberately acted in the way that he or she did;
2. see malicious intent in the other person's motives when none exists;
3. think that he or she is definitely in the right, whereas the other person is definitely wrong;
4. be incapable of seeing the other person's point of view; and
5. begin to hatch plots to exact revenge on the other person.

Action tendencies and response options

When a person is angry, his or her major action tendencies are as follows:

1. To attack the source of the frustration, rule-breaking or threat to self-esteem physically.
2. To attack the source of the frustration, rule-breaking or threat to self-esteem verbally.
3. To get back at the other person indirectly when the person is fearful (amongst other reasons) of making a direct attack.
4. To displace the attack, verbally and/or physically, onto another person (usually of lower status or less powerful than the original source and the attacker), an animal ('kicking the cat') or an object.
5. To withdraw angrily from the situation in which the frustration, rule-breaking or threat to self-esteem is occurring (as when the person 'storms out' of a meeting where someone is posing a threat to his or her self-esteem).
6. To tell others about the relevant incident with the intention of recruiting allies.

While the person is angry, he or she is not likely to choose response options that emphasise open, non-damning communication such as assertiveness. If he or she does attempt to communicate assertively when angry with the other person, then this form of healthy communication is likely to break down as soon as the other person continues to act in the same manner that originally triggered the person's anger-provoking irrational beliefs or as soon as that person indicates that he or she is critical of his or her assertiveness.

Annoyance: the healthy alternative to anger

According to rational-emotive psychology, annoyance (or non-demanding anger) is the healthy alternative to anger (or demanding anger). When a person is annoyed about being frustrated by another person, for example, he or she believes a version of one or more of the following rational beliefs:

1. I would much prefer it if you did not frustrate me, but there is no law of the universe which decrees that you absolutely should not have frustrated me.
2. It is bad that you frustrated me, but hardly terrible.
3. I can tolerate being frustrated by you, although I strongly dislike it.
4. You are not a rotten person for frustrating me, only a fallible human being who has done what I consider to be the wrong thing.

and when the other person's behaviour was previously (i.e. when he or she was angry) thought to constitute a threat to self-esteem:

5. I can accept myself as a fallible human being even when you may be implying that I am worthless.

When the person is annoyed, but not angry about being frustrated, observing another person violating one of the personal rules, or inferring that the other person is implying that he or she is worthless (or less worthy):

1. The person does not overestimate the extent to which the other person acted deliberately in the way that he or she did.
2. The person does not see malicious intent in the other person's motives when none exists.
3. The person does not think that he or she is definitely in the right, nor that the other person is definitely wrong.
4. The person is capable of seeing the other person's point of view.
5. The person does not mentally plot to exact revenge on the other person.

When the person is annoyed but not angry, there is an inclination to actualize his or her tendency to remain in the situation and deal with it constructively by choosing responses from the repertoire that include assertion and requesting (but not demanding) behavioural change from the other person.

Guilt

Here I consider guilt to be an unconstructive negative emotion, with remorse being its constructive negative counterpart (Dryden 1994).

Inferences

When a person feels guilty, he or she could be making one of three inferences. First, the consideration that he or she has violated one (or more) of his or her moral codes or ethical principles. This is known as the 'sin of commission'. Second, the consideration that he or she has failed to live up to one (or more) of his or her moral codes or ethical principles. This is known as the 'sin of omission'. Finally, he or she considers that, by his or her actions or inaction, the feelings of someone significant have been hurt. As mentioned several times already, whether or not he or she has actually violated a moral code, for example, is not the point. The important issue is that the person thinks that he or she has. This constitutes the A in the ABC of guilt.

Irrational beliefs

The rational-emotive psychology view of guilt is that it is based on the person's irrational beliefs about actual or inferred sins of commission, sins of omission or the infliction of hurt on a significant other. When a person feels guilty about violating one of the moral codes, for example, he or she believes a version of one or more of the following beliefs:

1. I must not violate my moral code.
2. It is awful that I violated my moral code.
3. It is unbearable that I have violated my moral code.
4. I am a bad person for violating my moral code and deserve to be punished.

Cognitive consequences of guilt

Once the person brings one or more of these irrational beliefs to the actual or inferred sin of commission, sin of omission or the sin of inflicting hurt on a significant other, in addition to creating guilt feelings, he or she will have a tendency to think in one or more of the following ways:

1. The person will tend to assume that she definitely has committed the sin.
2. The person will tend to assume more personal responsibility in the situation than is warranted.
3. The person will tend to assign far less responsibility to others than is warranted in the situation.
4. The person will tend not to think of mitigating factors which might help to explain the reasons for his or her behaviour (or lack of behaviour).

5. The person will tend to assume that he or she will receive some kind of retribution for such sinful behaviour.

Action tendencies and response options

When a person is feeling guilty, his or her major action tendencies are as follows:

1. To beg forgiveness from the person he or she considers has been wronged.
2. To promise unrealistically that he or she will not 'sin' again.
3. To punish him- or herself either physically or by depriving him- or herself of pleasure.
4. To anaesthetise him- or herself from the pain of guilt usually in self-defeating ways, e.g. by taking drugs or alcohol.
5. To disclaim responsibility for the wrongdoing, e.g. by claiming that he or she did not in fact 'sin, by making defensive excuses for his or her actions, or by blaming others for his or her behaviour.

When the person is feeling guilty, he or she is likely to choose response options which increase the likelihood that he or she will 'sin' in future. For example, if a person breaks a diet and feels guilty about it, he or she will tend to eat more for two reasons; first, to take away the pain of guilt and second, to actualise the 'I'm bad' belief, which is at the core of guilt. Here, because the person believes that he or she is a bad person for breaking the diet, he or she acts 'badly' (i.e. eats more) in accord with this belief. Given that he or she is feeling guilty and perpetuates her 'wrongdoing', the one thing that he or she does not do is to learn why the diet was broken in the first place. Given that he or she has not learned from this 'mistake', a repeat of this (i.e. breaking the diet) is more likely to happen in the future if similar circumstances exist.

Remorse: the healthy alternative to guilt

According to rational-emotive psychology, remorse is the healthy alternative to guilt. When a person is feeling remorseful about breaking one of the moral codes, for example, he or she believes a version of one or more of the following rational beliefs:

1. I would much prefer it if I would not violate my moral code, but there is no reason why I absolutely must not do so. Being human, I have no immunity from committing wrongdoings.
2. It is very unfortunate, but not awful that I violated my moral code.
3. Violating my moral code is difficult to tolerate, but it is not unbearable.

Common emotional problems

4. I am not a bad person for violating my moral code and therefore do not deserve to be punished. I am a fallible human being who has done the wrong thing.

When the person is feeling remorseful, but not guilty about 'sins' of commission or omission or about inflicting hurt on another person, that person will:

1. Not tend to assume that he or she definitely has committed the sin. Rather, he or she will look at the behaviour in context and with understanding, and will judge on that basis whether or not he or she has 'sinned'.
2. Not tend to assume more personal responsibility in the situation than is warranted, because he or she will look at all the factors involved and will only assume responsibility for that which falls within his or her sphere of direct influence.
3. Tend to assign responsibility to others for what falls within their sphere of direct influence in a given situation.
4. Tend to think of mitigating factors which might help to explain the reasons for his or her behaviour (or lack of behaviour).
5. Not assume that he or she will receive some kind of retribution for sinful behaviour.

When the person feels remorseful rather than guilty, there is an inclination to actualise his or her tendency:

1. To face up to the healthy pain that accompanies the realisation that he or she has violated a moral code, failed to live up to an ethical principle or inflicted hurt on someone close.
2. To ask for forgiveness from relevant others (rather than beg for it).
3. To undertake to understand why he or she acted in the way that he or she did, to learn from the experience and to resolve to put this learning into practice in future, relevant situations.
4. To atone for the 'sin' by taking some penalty.
5. To make amends to the person or persons that have been wronged.
6. To accept responsibility for the wrongdoing (e.g. by claiming that he or she did in fact 'sin', by refraining from making defensive excuses for these actions, or by refraining from blaming others for his or her behaviour.

Shame

Here I consider shame to be an unconstructive negative emotion, with regret being its constructive negative counterpart.

Inferences

When a person feels ashamed, he or she tends to infer that:

1. He or she has revealed something 'shameful' about him- or herself in public and that others will notice this and look down on him or her (and his or her family, for example) in some way (i.e. judge him or her or them negatively) and possibly shun him or her or them.
2. Somebody else has revealed something 'shameful' about the person in front of others or in a way that others will learn about, and these others will look down on the person (and his or her family) and possibly shun him or her or them.
3. A person, persons or social group with whom he or she closely identifies within his or her personal domain have revealed something 'shameful' about themselves in public, and that others will notice this and look down on them and the person him- or herself (i.e. judge them negatively) and possibly shun them.
4. Something 'shameful' has been revealed about a person, persons or social group with whom he or she closely identifies within his or her personal domain, and that this has been done in front of others or in a way such that others will learn about, and these others will look down on them and the person and possibly shun them.

What constitutes 'shameful' here will depend heavily on the norms and mores of the judging social group. Thus, one person may consider being caught having an affair with a married man as 'shameful', while another person may consider it 'shameful' if his daughter marries a man outside of their caste. In addition, in shame, the actual presence of the judging group is less important than their psychological presence in the person's mind.

Irrational beliefs

The rational-emotive psychology view of shame is that it is based on the person's irrational beliefs about the actual, or inferred, discovery of 'shameful' information about the person and/or others with whom he or she closely identifies, and any associated negative evaluations of self and others that the judging group actually makes or, more frequently, is thought to make. When a person feels ashamed about revealing a personal weakness in public, for example, he or she believes a version of one or more of the following beliefs:

1a. I must not reveal a weakness in public and
1b. I must not incur the disapproval of others.
2a. It is awful that I revealed a weakness in public and

2b. It is awful that others disapprove of me.
3a. It is unbearable that I revealed a weakness in public and
3b. It is unbearable that others disapprove of me.
4a. I am an inadequate, defective person for revealing a weakness in public.
4b. If others look down on me for revealing a weakness in public, then they are right about me. I am an insignificant, inadequate defect.

Cognitive consequences of shame

Once the person brings one or more of these irrational beliefs to the actual or inferred public disclosure of 'shameful' information about his- or herself or a closely identified reference group, in addition to creating feelings of shame he or she will have a tendency to think in one or more of the following ways:

1. The person will tend to overestimate the 'shamefulness' of the information revealed.
2. The person will tend to overestimate the likelihood that the judging group will notice or take an interest in this information.
3. The person will tend to overestimate the degree of public disapproval that he or she and/or his or her reference group will receive (assuming that he or she and/or they will incur some disapproval).
4. The person will tend to overestimate the length of time that the judging group will remember the 'shameful' information and the length of time that they will continue to disapprove of him or her and/or the reference group.
5. The person will tend to overestimate the likelihood that he or she and/or the reference group will be shunned by the judging group.
6. The person will tend to overestimate the length of time that the judging group will shun him or her and/or the reference group (assuming that they will be shunned for a period).

Action tendencies and response options

When a person is feeling ashamed, the major action tendencies are as follows:

1. To remove oneself from the 'gaze' of the actual or inferred judging group either by avoiding eye contact (the lowering of one's gaze in shame), by wishing that he or she was elsewhere (wanting the 'ground to open up and swallow me') or by physically withdrawing from the social arena.
2. To isolate oneself from others.
3. To save face by attacking the person or persons who have 'shamed'

oneself and/or one's reference group, either physically or verbally.
4. To head off disapproval or ridicule by disarming the judging group in some way (e.g. by severely condemning oneself in order to elicit sympathy from the judging group).
5. To defend one's threatened self-esteem (e.g. by arguing with the person or persons who are 'shaming' him or her – many domestic arguments occur as a result of one or both parties defending themselves against shame).
6. To ignore attempts by others to restore the social equilibrium.

When the person is feeling ashamed, he or she is not likely to choose response options that will connect him or her to the social group. Indeed, if advantage is not taken of the attempts that others may make to re-integrate him or her into the social group, the person may attract further social disapproval.

Before I consider the healthy alternative to shame, let me say a word about embarrassment. When embarrassment is based on irrational beliefs, it occurs when the person makes an inference that a personal weakness has been revealed that is less 'shameful' than in shame, or when a compliment is received that he or she believes he or she does not deserve. This latter inference is usually not present in shame.

Regret: the healthy alternative to shame

According to rational-emotive psychology, regret is the healthy alternative to shame. REP's view of regret here is that it is based on the person's rational beliefs about the actual or inferred discovery of 'shameful' information about the person and/or others with whom he or she closely identifies, and any associated negative evaluations of self and others that the judging group actually makes or, more frequently, is thought to make. When a person feels regret (but not ashamed) about revealing a personal weakness in public, for example, he or she believes a version of one or more of the following rational beliefs:

1a. I would prefer not to reveal a weakness in public, but there is no reason why I must not do so and
1b. I would prefer not to incur the disapproval of others, but there is no reason why they must not disapprove of me.
2a. It is bad that I revealed a weakness in public, but it is not the end of the world and
2b. It is bad, but not terrible that others disapprove of me.
3a. Revealing a weakness in public is difficult to withstand, but it not intolerable and
3b. I find the disapproval of others difficult to bear, but I can withstand it.

4a. I am certainly not an inadequate, defective person for revealing a weakness in public. Rather, I am a fallible, unrateable human being for doing so and
4b. If others look down on me for revealing a weakness in public and think that I am an insignificant, inadequate defect, then they are wrong about me. I may have my defects, but I am not a defect. Rather, I am a fallible human being with strengths, weaknesses and neutral aspects.

When the person is feeling regret about revealing a weakness in public, but not ashamed about it, there will be a tendency to think in one or more of the following ways:

1. The person will tend not to overestimate the 'shamefulness' of the information revealed. Rather, he or she will see it in a compassionate, self-accepting context.
2. The person will tend not to overestimate the likelihood that the judging group will notice or take an interest in this information. Rather, he or she will consider the degree of 'shamefulness' of the revealed weakness and what he or she knows about the views of the judging group in determining the likelihood that they will be interested in such a revelation.
3. Following on from the above, the person will tend not to overestimate the degree of public disapproval that the person and/or the reference group will receive (assuming that he or she and/or they will incur some disapproval).
4. For the same reason, the person will tend not to overestimate the length of time that the judging group will remember the 'shameful' information and the length of time that they will continue to disapprove of the person and/or the reference group.
5. As feelings of regret encourage the person to take a more objective view of his or her weakness and the judging group's reaction to it, he or she will not tend to overestimate the likelihood that the person and/or his or her reference group will be shunned by the judging group and
6. Similarly, the person will not tend to overestimate the length of time that the judging group will shun the person and/or his or her reference group (assuming that they will be shunned for a period).

When the person is regretful but not ashamed, he or she tends to actualise the tendency to continue to participate actively in social interaction. Thus, he or she may choose to focus on the humour implicit in the event if this is appropriate (without playing the clown) or to apologise without desperation for inconveniencing others, if this has been the case. The person is also able to utilise the attempts of others to help restore the social equilibrium. Finally, the person is able to stand up for him- or herself, and the reference group, in the face of any social disapproval, because the person can accept him- or herself, and members of the reference group, as fallible human beings who can hold their heads up high even though they may have revealed (or had revealed by another) negative aspects of themselves to others.

Hurt

Here I consider hurt to be an unconstructive negative emotion, with disappointment being its constructive negative counterpart.

Inferences

When a person feels hurt, he or she tends to infer that a significant other has acted towards him or her in an unfair manner, or that he or she has been treated by the significant other in a way that was not deserved. As elsewhere, the person's inferences may be correct or incorrect and thus, they need to be tested against observable reality as far as this can be done.

The other's behaviour, about which a person may feel hurt, tends to fall into two major categories: acts of commission, and acts of omission. Examples of acts of commission include betrayal, being unfairly criticised, disapproval and rejection; examples of acts of omission include neglect, being ignored or excluded, not being appreciated and not having reasonable desires met.

Irrational beliefs

The rational-emotive psychology view of hurt is that it is based on the person's irrational beliefs about the actual or inferred unfair treatment that he or she has received at the hands of a significant other (or others), particularly when he or she infers that such treatment was undeserved. When a person feels hurt about being treated unfairly by his or her partner, for example, he or she believes a version of one or more of the following irrational beliefs:

1. I must not get the treatment from him that I do not deserve.
2. It's terrible that he has treated me unfairly.
3. I cannot stand it when he treats me unfairly.
4a. Perhaps I am less deserving if he treats me in the way that he does; and/or
4b. Poor me for being treated so unfairly.

Cognitive consequences of hurt

Once the person brings one or more of these irrational beliefs to the actual or inferred unfair treatment at the hands of a significant other, in addition to creating hurt feelings, he or she will have a tendency to think in one or more of the following ways:

1. The person will tend to overestimate the unfairness of the other person's behaviour towards him or her.
2. The person will tend to think of the other person as showing a lack of care or indifference to his or her feelings
3. The person will tend to think of him- or herself as alone, uncared for and misunderstood.
4. The person will tend to think of past hurts and upsets inflicted on him or her by that person and by others.
5. The person will tend to think that whosoever has 'hurt' him or her has to do something to put things right of his or her own accord (i.e. without needing prompting from the hurt person or anyone else), before the hurt person raises the issue with him.

Action tendencies and response options

When a person is feeling hurt, the major action tendencies are as follows:

1. To close down communication channels with the person who has 'hurt' him or her. This is colloquially known as sulking. In a book that I wrote on this subject entitled *The Incredible Sulk* (Dryden, 1992), I distinguished between silent sulking (where the person withdraws into his- or herself) and aggressive sulking (where the person moves around slamming and banging doors, for example). In that book, I identified the following six purposes of sulking:
    * To punish the other;
    * To get what the person wants;
    * To get the other to make the first move;
    * To extract proof of caring from the other;
    * To protect the person from further hurt; and
    * To restore power.

   I recommend the interested reader to consult this book for a more detailed discussion of sulking and its purposes.
2. To criticise the other person, normally without disclosing what he or she feels hurt about.

As hurt often overlaps with anger and depression, it is possible to speak of 'depressed hurt' and 'angry hurt'. As such, the action tendencies associated with depression and anger are relevant in 'depressed hurt' and 'angry hurt' respectively.

Disappointment: the healthy alternative to hurt

According to rational-emotive psychology, disappointment is the healthy alternative to hurt. REP's view of disappointment here is that it is based on the person's rational beliefs about the actual or inferred unfair treatment that he or she has received at the hands of a significant other (or others), particularly when he or she infers that such treatment was undeserved. When, for example, a woman feels disappointment about being treated unfairly by her partner, she believes a version of one or more of the following rational beliefs:

1. I would prefer not to get the treatment from him that I do not deserve, but there is no reason why I must not get what I don't deserve.
2. It is bad that he has treated me unfairly, but it is not terrible that he has acted in this way towards me.
3. I can withstand it when he treats me unfairly, although it is difficult to put up with.
4a. I am not less deserving if he treats me in the way that he does. I am the same fallible human being whether he treats me fairly or unfairly; and/or
4b. I am not a poor creature to be pitied for being treated so unfairly. Rather I am a person who is in a poor situation.

When this woman is disappointed, but not hurt, about being treated unfairly by a significant other, she will have a tendency to think in one or more of the following ways:

1. She will not tend to overestimate the unfairness of the other person's behaviour towards her. Rather, she will be more able to look at his behaviour from his point of view than when she is feeling hurt, and will see it in a wider, less egocentric context.
2. She will be less likely to think of the other person as showing a lack of care or indifference to her feelings than when feeling hurt. If, however, there is evidence for his uncaringness when she is feeling disappointed about this, she will be more able to see that he can care for her in general, while still be uncaring on this specific occasion than when she is feeling hurt.
3. She will not tend to think of herself as alone, uncared for and misunderstood, although if the evidence exists, she will consider that she has been treated badly.
4. She will be less likely to think of past hurts and upsets inflicted on

her by that person and by others than when she is feeling hurt.
5. She will not tend to think that the person who has acted unfairly towards her has to do something to put things right of his own accord (i.e. without needing prompting from her or anyone else), before she brings the issue up with him.

When the person is feeling disappointed but not hurt, she tends to choose options from her response repertoire which actualise her action tendency to influence the other person to act in a 'fairer' manner. Thus, she will communicate her feelings clearly, directly and assertively to the other person.

Jealousy

Here I consider jealousy to be an unconstructive negative emotion, with 'concern for one's relationship' being its constructive negative counterpart. Jealousy involves a three-person relationship involving the person, a significant other and a third person. Jealousy is frequently confused with envy, which is discussed later in this chapter.

Inferences

When a person feels jealous, he or she tends to infer that there is a threat to his or her relationship with a significant other.

Irrational beliefs

The rational-emotive psychology view of jealousy is that it is based on the person's irrational beliefs about an actual or inferred threat to his or her relationship with a significant other. When, for example, a woman feels jealous about such a threat to her relationship with her partner, she believes a version of one or more of the following irrational beliefs:

1. I must be sure that there is no threat to my relationship with my partner. It would be terrible if I did not have such certainty. Such uncertainty is intolerable.
2. My partner must only be interested in me. It would be terrible if he showed an interest in another woman. I could not stand that. If he did show interest in another woman it would prove that (a) he is rotten and (b) I am worthless.
3. No other woman must show any interest in my partner. It would be terrible if one did. I could not bear that. If a woman did show interest in my partner it would prove that (a) she is no good and (b) I am worthless.

Cognitive consequences of jealousy

Once this person brings one or more of these irrational beliefs to the actual or inferred threat to her relationship with her partner, in addition to creating jealous feelings, she will have a tendency to think in one or more of the following ways:

1. She will tend to see threats to her relationship when none objectively can be said to exist.
2. She will be thinking constantly that the loss of her relationship is imminent.
3. She will misconstrue ordinary conversation between her partner and other women as having romantic or sexual connotations.
4. She will construct visual images of imagined scenarios in which her partner is involved with other women and she will think that these scenarios are real.
5. If her partner does admit to finding another woman attractive, then she believes that (a) he finds that woman more attractive than her, (b) that he wants to have a relationship with this woman, and (c) he will leave her for this other woman.

These inferences will then serve as new activating events (A's), which will trigger a new set of irrational beliefs, which, in turn, will deepen the person's jealous feelings.

Action tendencies and response options

When, using this example, the woman is feeling jealous, her major action tendencies are as follows:

1. To monitor the actions and sentiments of her partner with respect to his feelings about her and other women (e.g. constantly asking her partner for assurances that he loves her and that he has no interest in other women, phoning her partner at work to check on his movements).
2. To search for evidence that her partner is involved with someone else (e.g. checking his car for signs of the presence of another woman and cross-examining him for signs of involvement with other women).
3. To attempt to restrict the movements and activities of her partner (e.g. by not allowing him to go to pubs with his friends because of the presence of other women or switching off the television when attractive women are on the screen).
4. To set tests which her partner has to pass (e.g. inviting attractive women to meet her partner and then monitoring his reactions

closely to ensure that he shows no interest in these women).
5. To retaliate (e.g. becoming sexually involved with another man to 'get even' with her partner for his actual or, more frequently, his presumed infidelity).
6. To sulk (refusing to talk to her partner because of his presumed interest in other women).

Concern for the relationship: the healthy alternative to jealousy

According to rational-emotive psychology, concern for one's relationship is the healthy alternative to jealousy. REP's view of such concern is that it is based on the person's rational beliefs about the actual or inferred threat to his or her relationship. When, for example, a woman feels concerned about a threat to her relationship with her partner, she believes a version of one or more of the following rational beliefs:

1. I would like to be sure that there is no threat to my relationship with my partner, but I do not have to have such certainty. It would be bad, but not terrible if I did not have such assurance. Such uncertainty is difficult to put up with, but not intolerable.
2. It would be nice if my partner were only interested in me, but there is no reason why he has to show such exclusive interest. It would be unfortunate if he showed an interest in another woman, but it would not be terrible. It would be difficult to tolerate if he did show interest in another woman, but I could withstand it. If he did show such interest it would neither prove that he is rotten nor that I am worthless. He is a fallible human being who would be doing the wrong thing and my worth to myself is not dependent on my partner showing me exclusive interest. I can accept myself unconditionally.
3. I would prefer it if no other woman were to show interest in my partner. It would be bad but not terrible if one did. This would be difficult to tolerate, but I could bear it. If a woman did show interest in my partner it would neither prove that she is no good nor that I am worthless. She is a fallible human being who would be doing the wrong thing and again my worth to myself is not dependent on whether or not a woman shows interest in my partner. I can accept myself unconditionally.

When this woman is concerned about a threat to her relationship but not jealous about it, she will have a tendency to think in one or more of the following ways:

1. She will not tend to see threats to her relationship when none can objectively be said to exist.

2. She will not constantly think that the loss of her relationship is imminent. Rather, because she trusts her partner, she will think that he will probably neither initiate a relationship with another woman nor respond to advances from another woman.
3. She will not misconstrue ordinary conversation between her partner and other women as having romantic or sexual connotations. Rather, she will see it as an ordinary conversation.
4. She will not construct visual images of imagined scenarios in which her partner is involved with other women or if she does, she will not think that these scenarios are real.
5. If her partner does admit to finding another woman attractive then she neither believes that he finds this woman more attractive than her nor that he wants to have a relationship with the woman. She accepts that people in a relationship can still find other people attractive and that this is a fact of life. She will not make more of this unless she has evidence to the contrary.

When the person, such as the woman in this example, is concerned about her relationship but not jealous, there is an inclination to choose the following behaviours from her response repertoire. The woman allows her partner to express his feelings without constantly asking for reassurance that he loves her. She does not keep asking him about his feelings for other women, nor does she monitor his whereabouts, look for evidence that he is involved with someone else or cross-examine him about such involvements. She allows her partner freedom of movement and does not try to stop him looking at other women. Furthermore, she does not set him tests to gauge his interest in other women.

If she does have evidence that her partner is involved with someone else, she will express her distress assertively and without anger, do something effective to try to win him back (if that is what she wants), and ask her partner to set healthy limits on his outside involvements if their relationship is to continue. If her partner leaves her, she will strive to reorganise her life constructively after a period of healthy grief.

Envy

The final unconstructive negative emotion I will consider in this chapter is envy. There is no acceptable word, from an REP point of view, to denote a healthy alternative to envy. Consequently, I will distinguish between healthy envy and unhealthy envy and begin by discussing unhealthy envy.

Inferences

When a person feels envious, he or she infers that another person (or group of people) possesses and enjoys something desirable (e.g. a quality, an object or a relationship) that he or she does not have.

Irrational beliefs

The rational-emotive psychology view of unhealthy envy is that it is based on the person's irrational beliefs about the actual or inferred desired, but unpossessed, quality, relationship or object. When a person feels envious towards another person for possessing a desired object, for example, he or she believes a version of one or more of the following irrational beliefs:

1a. I must have what he has.
2a. It is terrible that I don't have what he has.
3a. I cannot stand the deprivation.
4a. Not having what he has makes me less worthy than him.

The above irrational beliefs reflect the situation where the person demands that he or she has to have what the other person has. The following irrational beliefs relate to a different situation, i.e. where the person demands that the other person must not have what he or she does not have. Here, the person does not want what the other has. Rather, he or she wants the desired object to be taken away from the other person.

1b. He must not have what I do not have.
2b. It is terrible if he has what I do not have.
3b. I cannot stand the situation where he has what I do not have.
4b. He is more worthy than I am because he has what I don't have.

Cognitive consequences of unhealthy envy

Once the person brings one or more of these irrational beliefs to the actual or inferred situation where another person (or group of people) possesses and enjoys something desirable (e.g. a quality, an object or a relationship) that he or she does not have, in addition to creating feelings of unhealthy envy, she will have a tendency to think in one or more of the following ways:

1. The person will tend to denigrate in his or her mind the value of the desired possession.
2. The person will tend to convince him- or herself, if he or she has nothing similar to the desired possession, that he or she is happy with the possessions that he or she has (although in reality this is not so).

3. The person will tend to convince him- or herself that the possessions that he or she has which are similar to the desired possession are just as good or even superior to that which is owned by the other person.
4. The person will tend to think about how to obtain the desired possession (either that very one or one similar), whether it is really useful to him or her or not.
5. The person will tend to think about how to deprive the other person of his possession.

Action tendencies and response options

When a person is feeling unhealthy envy, his or her major action tendencies are as follows:

1. To disparage verbally the person who has the desired possession.
2. To disparage verbally the desired possession.
3. To take away the desired possession from the other person (either so that he or she will have it or so that the other person is deprived of it).
4. To spoil or destroy the desired possession so that the other person does not have it.

Healthy envy: the constructive alternative to unhealthy envy

According to rational-emotive psychology, healthy envy is the constructive alternative to unhealthy envy. REP's view of healthy envy here is that it is based on the person's rational beliefs about the actual or inferred situation where another person (or group of people) possesses and enjoys something desirable (e.g. a quality, an object or a relationship) that he or she does not have. When a person feels healthily envious towards another person for possessing a desired object, for example, he or she believes a version of one or more of the following rational beliefs:

1a. I would like to have what he has, but there is no reason why I must have it.
2a. It is bad, but not terrible that I do not have what he has.
3a. I can withstand the deprivation, although it is difficult to put up with.
4a. Not having what he has does not make me less worthy than him. I am equal to him in humanity whether or not I have what he has.

The above rational beliefs reflect the situation where the person wants to have what the other person has (but does not demand that he or she must have it). The following rational beliefs again relate to a different situation, i.e. where the person prefers that the other person not have what he or she does not have (but does not demand that this must be the case). Here, as before, the person does not want what the other has, rather, he or she wants the desired object to be taken away from the other person.

1b. I would prefer it if he does not have what I do not have, but there is no reason why he must not have it.
2b. It is bad, but not terrible if he has what I do not have.
3b. I can withstand the situation where he has what I do not have, although frankly it is difficult to bear.
4b. He is not more worthy than I am because he has what I do not have. We are both fallible human beings, equal in humanity although unequal in this respect.

When the person is healthily envious about an actual or inferred situation where another person (or group of people) possesses and enjoys something desirable (e.g. a quality, an object or a relationship) that he or she does not have, the person will have a tendency to think in one or more of the following ways:

1. The person will not tend to denigrate in his or her mind the value of the desired possession. Rather, he or she will honestly admit that he or she does desire it (if this is truly the case).
2. The person will not tend to convince him- or herself, if he or she has nothing similar to the desired possession, that he or she is happy with the possessions that he or she has. Again, the person will honestly admit to him- or herself that he or she does desire it (if this is truly the case).
3. The person will not tend to convince him- or herself that the possessions that he or she has which are similar to the desired possession are just as good or even superior to what the other person has, if this is truly the case.
4. The person will tend to think about how to obtain the desired possession (either that very one or one similar), because he or she truly desires it for healthy reasons.
5. The person will not tend to think about how to deprive the other person of his possession. He or she can allow him to have this possession and think objectively whether it is truly what he or she wants

When the person is healthily envious, he or she tends to choose options from the response repertoire which actualise the action tendency to obtain the desired possession if it is truly what he or she wants.

Meta-emotional problems

When we have an emotional experience, we tend to have feelings about that experience. I call these feelings meta-emotions – a term which literally means 'emotions about emotions'. In addition, we have emotional problems about our emotional problems. I call these meta-emotional problems. In this section, I discuss the most frequently occurring meta-emotional problems. As part of the discussion, I also identify the beliefs that tend to underpin these meta-emotional problems.

Guilt about anger

You will remember that when a person experiences guilt, one of three inferences are made: (1) 'I have broken my moral code', (2) 'I have failed to act according to one of my ethical principles', or (3) 'I have hurt or harmed someone'. When a person feels guilty about his or her anger, this guilt may be about one, or more, of four things:

1. The feeling of anger (where the person's moral code forbids even the experience of anger).
2. The expression of anger (where the person's moral code allows the experience of anger, but forbids the expression of it).
3. Failure to act ethically (here the person's anger serves to remind that there has been a failure to act ethically in the situation where he or she experienced angry feelings, e.g. with compassionate understanding.
4. The consequences of the expressed anger (here the person assesses the damage others may have suffered as a result of this expressed anger and makes him- or herself guilty if it can be concluded that he or she has hurt or harmed someone).

However, as you will no doubt recall from Chapters 2, 4 and 5, while inferences give shape to the person's emotional experience (in this case they point to guilt or remorse), they do not determine whether the person experiences the unhealthy negative emotion (in this case guilt) or the healthy alternative (in this case remorse). It is the person's beliefs that are central to determining which type of emotion is experienced by the person (see pp.90–93) for a review of the beliefs that underpin guilt and remorse).

In Figure 7.1, I present an ABC analysis of an example in which a person experiences anger (the primary emotional problem) and guilt over this anger (the secondary emotional problem, or what I prefer to call, the meta-emotional problem).

Common emotional problems

A1: A person jumped the queue in front of me while I was waiting for a bus

B1: He absolutely should not have done that

C1: Anger [expressed by shouting at the other person]

A2: I lost my temper in public (moral code violation)

B2: I must not show my anger in public. I am something of a bad person for doing so on this occasion.

C2: Guilt

Figure 7.1 An example of guilt about anger

Anxiety about anxiety

Anxiety about anxiety is quite a common meta-emotional problem. It is a central feature in panic attacks (see Chapter 8) and so-called 'free floating' anxiety. As will be shown in the next chapter, when a person infers that there is a threat to his or her ego, or to his or her sense of discomfort, and holds an irrational belief about this threat, the interaction between the inferred A and the irrational belief leads him or her to make a further inference which is likely to be more negative than the first inference (see the example in Figure 7.2). The person then brings another irrational belief to this new inference and creates an even more negative inference as a result. I will demonstrate this important ingredient of anxiety about anxiety in Figure 8.1.

A1: I might go blank while reading my essay in class.

B1: I must not go blank and if I did it would be terrible. I would make a fool of myself.

C1: Anxiety

A2: Anxiety

B2: I must not get anxious. I can't stand the feeling of anxiety.

C2: Increased anxiety

A3: I may pass out.

Figure 7.2. An example of anxiety about anxiety.

A1: My wife is showing an interest in another man

B1: She must only be interested in me. I can't bear to see her talking to another man.

C2: Jealousy

A2: Jealousy is a sign of immaturity which others will be able to spot in me

B2: 1. I must not be so immature and I am less worthy if I act in such a childish fashion.
2. Others must not see this side of me. If they do then I will lose their respect which will prove that I am inadequate.

C2: Shame

Figure 7.3. An Example of Shame about Jealousy

Shame about jealousy

Shame often serves as a meta-emotion. This happens when the person infers that his primary emotion represents some kind of weakness such as immaturity (see Figure 7.3) or a failure in self-control. As I discussed earlier in this chapter, shame frequently involves the person making an inference about the reaction of an actual or presumed audience to his or her revealed weakness.

Having considered several common emotional and meta-emotional problems, in the following and final chapter of the book, I discuss some of the ways in which A's, B's and C's interact with one another, often in complex ways.

Chapter 8
Complex relationships among the ABC's of rational-emotive psychology

In Chapter 2, I gave a brief overview of the ABC's of rational-emotive psychology and in subsequent chapters I considered each element separately. Thus, in Chapter 3, I discussed inferred, interpreted and actual activating events which taken together represent A; in Chapter 4, I detailed the REP position on evaluative beliefs at B; while in Chapters 5 and 6, I considered the emotional and behavioural consequences at C of holding evaluative beliefs at B. Finally, in Chapter 7, I brought this material together and outlined the ABC's of common emotional problems. In that chapter, I began to detail some of the complex relationships that can occur among the ABC's without making this explicit. In this chapter, I will be more specific in detailing some of the complex relationships and interactions that can exist among actual events, interpretations and inferences of these events, evaluative beliefs, emotions, action tendencies and behaviour.*

To make a complex situation even more complicated we also have to consider a person's goals or purposes, which Albert Ellis (1991) calls G's. As I have not yet discussed goals in this book, I begin by considering them and how they influence and are influenced by the ABC's of REP. I call this process of mutual influence 'reciprocal influence', and I consider various types of reciprocal influence throughout this chapter.

Reciprocal influence I: how goals (G's) influence and are influenced by the ABC's of REP

People bring their goals and purposes (G's) to the ABC's of their experience and these goals have an influence on the ABC's. In turn, their goals can be influenced by these ABC's. Thus, if a person has the goal

---
* A full discussion of all possible interactions would merit a volume on its own. Consequently, I will discuss a sample of such interactions in this chapter.

of achieving promotion at work, this goal will effect and be affected by his ABC's in the following illustrative ways.

G's and actual A's

The person's goal (G) of achieving promotion at work will influence the actual events (A's) that he or she chooses to create and encounter. Thus, a man may choose to stay late at work (i.e. he creates and encounters more work-oriented A's); he may refuse to go to the pub after work with his friends (i.e. he creates and encounters less socially-oriented A's); and he may run into conflict with his wife who complains to him that she and her children are being deprived of his company (i.e. he creates and encounters more stressful family-related A's). The more important his goal of achieving promotion is to him, the more likely it is that he will create and encounter these actual A's.

In addition, this man's goals are influenced by actual A's. For example, if he consistently is rejected for promotion at work, eventually he may well relinquish this goal. Whether he thinks rationally or irrationally about these rejections will, of course, have a mediating effect on whether he persists with or relinquishes his goal. However, independent of his beliefs, the more actual rejections he gets, the more likely it is that he will relinquish his goal.

G's and inferred A's

The man's promotion aspirations (G) will also influence the types of inferences that he makes about actual events. For example, if his manager praises him for a piece of work that he has done (actual A), he may make the inference 'This means that he will put in a good word for me with the boss.' Whereas, if his manager criticises him for the piece of work, he may infer 'My manager won't support my application for promotion.' The more important his goal of achieving promotion is to him, the more likely it will be that he will make these inferences and the more he will consider these inferences to be facts.

In turn, a person's goal will be influenced by the types of inferences that he or she makes. For example, the more positive the inferences, the more important the goal is likely to become. Conversely, the more negative the inferences, the more likely it is that he or she will relinquish or change the goals (e.g. by setting his or her sights lower). Again this process will be influenced by the type of beliefs held about these inferences, but independent of what he or she believes the relationship as stated between the impact of inferences on the person's goals tends to exist.

G's and B's

When a man, for example, has the goal of achieving promotion at work, this goal influences the type of beliefs that the person has about whether or not he achieves this goal. If he does achieve it, he may believe rationally: 'It is good that I have been promoted, but it doesn't make me a better person', or irrationally: 'It is wonderful that I have been promoted. What a great person I am'. However, if he fails to realize his goal, he may rationally believe: 'It is unfortunate that I haven't been promoted. I am still a fallible human being though', or irrationally conclude: 'It is terrible that I failed to get my promotion. What a worthless person I am.'

The more important the person's goal of obtaining promotion is to him, the stronger his rational beliefs will be (if he thinks rationally about his goal) and the more rigid will be his irrational beliefs (if he thinks irrationally about his goal).

In general, a person's goals (G's) do not lead the person to have beliefs of indifference, e.g. 'It doesn't matter if I am promoted or not.' If the person does have such a belief, it is usually a defence against the unhealthy negative emotions that stem from his irrational beliefs, rather than as a direct result of his goals.

Goals are, in turn, affected by the type of beliefs the person holds about his job promotion. Thus, if a person holds irrational beliefs about the promotion, he is more likely to relinquish or modify this goal than if he holds a set of rational beliefs about it. This is true especially if he encounters (or creates) negative actual A's or makes negative inferences.

The impact of G's on emotional C's

When a person has the goal of achieving a job promotion, as in the above example, then this will have an impact on his emotions at C, although usually this will occur as a result of the interaction between his goals and the types of beliefs that he holds about the promotion. Thus, if he thinks rationally about the sought after promotion (G), he will experience healthy positive feelings about the promotion if he obtains it (or if it looks as if he will obtain it) – e.g. pleasure, joy, or eagerness, or he will experiece healthy negative feelings if he does not obtain it (or if it looks as if he will not obtain it) – e.g. disappointment, sadness and concern. The intensity of these healthy feelings will depend on the degree of importance of the person's goal and the strength of conviction he has in his rational beliefs. For example, the person will experience strong feelings of sadness when he fails to achieve his promotion if this goal is important to him and if his conviction in his rational belief is strong.

However, if he thinks irrationally about the sought after promotion (G), he will experience unhealthy positive feelings about the promotion if he obtains it (or if it looks as if he will obtain it) – e.g. mania, or he will experience unhealthy negative feelings if he does not obtain it (or if it looks as if he will not obtain it) – e.g. hurt, depression and anxiety.

Again, the intensity of these unhealthy feelings will depend on the degree of importance of the person's goal and the degree of rigidity with which he holds irrational beliefs. For example, the person will experience strong feelings of depression when he fails to achieve his promotion if this goal is important to him and if he rigidly adheres to his irrational belief.

Turning to the influence of a person's emotions on his goals, it is probably the case that when the person is feeling positive, then he will maintain or even increase the sense of importance that he gives to his goal of achieving promotion at work. If he is feeling manic (which is a positive unhealthy emotion), he will tend to consider his goal all important, while if he is feeling very pleased (which is a positive healthy emotion) he will tend to consider his goal to be important, but not all important. Similarly, if he experiences an unhealthy negative emotion he will think of his goal as either all important (when feeling anxious) or unimportant (when feeling depressed). Whereas if he experiences a healthy negative emotion, e.g. concern or sadness, he will still consider his goal to be important, but not crucial.

G's and behavioural C's

When the person has the goal of achieving a job promotion, this has a decided impact on his or her behaviour. The following behaviours are illustrative of this impact and need to be compared with the situation where the person does not have this goal. There will be a tendency to:

- work harder;
- seek allies who can help him or her to achieve the goal;
- take more care over work;
- be more punctual about arriving at work on time;
- volunteer for extra work;
- stay at work later than his or her scheduled leaving time;
- find ways of showing the boss how well and how hard he or she is doing.

There are other salient issues that are important to take into account here. These include the importance of the person's goal and the nature of his or her beliefs about achieving that goal.

Thus, the more important the goal is to the person, the more likely it is that he or she will act in the ways illustrated above, and the more effort that will be invested in these activities. In addition, the constructive implementation of these activities is dependent to a large (but not exclusive degree) on the type of beliefs that the person holds about achieving the goal. Thus if a rational belief is held about achieving the goal (e.g. 'I would like to be promoted at work, but there is no reason why I must achieve my goal'), then rational-emotive psychology would hypothesise that he or she will be more subtle and more successful at implementing the behavioural strategies listed above than if an irrational belief is held about goal achievement (e.g. 'I absolutely have to obtain my promotion'). As noted in Chapter 4, rational beliefs tend to promote constructive, goal-seeking behaviour, while irrational beliefs tend to impede such behaviour.

Alternatively, a person's behaviour can influence his or her goals. Thus, if the person works hard at the job, this will tend to reinforce the importance of the goal of achieving promotion, wheres if he or she procrastinates or shirks at the duties, such behaviour will tend to weaken the importance of the goal.

Reciprocal influence II: how actual A's influence and are influenced by inferred A's and B's

Actual activating events (actual A's) are events that occur in reality. They are distinguished from inferred events in that they do not contain any of the person's inferences which add meaning to the event. Actual events interact with a person's inferences, beliefs, emotions, behaviours and goals in complex ways. I will give some examples below to illustrate this complexity.

Actual A's and inferred A's

The relationship between actual and inferred A's are often influenced by the person's goals. Thus, when a person has a goal such as a job promotion then he or she is likely to infer that certain actual A's will help to achieve the goals, while other actual A's will impede the quest to achieve his or her goal. The more important is the goal, the more likely it is that the person will make such inferences.

The more negative an event is, the more likely it is that the person will make negative inferences about that event and the more distorted these negative inferences are likely to be.† This explains why people often are faced with a double dose of negativity at A – one related to the actual event and the other related to his or her inferences.

Let me take rape as an example. Being raped is obviously a very negative activating event for the vast majority of people. As such, it will

---

†This is generally the case if we assume that the person's beliefs are held constant. As we see later, a person's beliefs can augment or minimize the chances that he or she will make distorted negative inferences about actual A's.

strongly influence those who have been raped to make highly distorted negative inferences such as 'I'll never get over the experience', 'I'm much more likely to be raped again' and 'It was my fault'. In saying this, I am neither condoning the crime of rape nor blaming the victim for making such inferences. All I am doing is pointing out that when people face very negative actual events, it is highly likely that they will make distorted negative inferences about these actual A's.

The type of inferences a person makes can influence the actual A's to which a person pays attention. For example, if a person infers that there is a good chance that he or she will be promoted at work, then he or she is more likely to pay attention to actual A's that are consistent with such an inference (e.g. instances of people complimenting his or her work) than to actual A's that are inconsistent with this inference (e.g. when the person's work is ignored or criticised). This pattern is reversed when the person infers that there is a poor chance that he or she will gain promotion. This effect is accentuated if the person holds an irrational belief about promotion, and attenuated if he or she holds a rational belief.

Actual A's and B's

Actual A's can influence the type of beliefs a person holds, and a similar point can be made with respect to the impact of actual A's on beliefs to that made above about the impact of actual A's on inferred A's. Namely, the more negative the actual A, the more likely it is that the person will think irrationally about it. Thus, if a person encounters a mildly negative or moderately negative actual A, then he or she may hold a version of the following rational belief: 'I would prefer it if this event had not occurred, but there's no reason why it absolutely should not have happened.' However, if the person encounters a highly negative actual A, then it is more likely that he or she will hold a version of the following irrational belief than if faced with a less negative actual A: 'Because I really don't want this event to occur, therefore it absolutely should not happen.'

When highly negative events do happen to people, these A's often trigger interesting irrationalities in these people which would be triggered less frequently by less aversive actual A's. Some people irrationally believe, for example, that when they experience an adversity: 'It must only be a small one', or 'It absolutely should not have been as bad as it is.' Such people believe that they absolutely should be immune from such highly aversive actual A's. This is often what underlies the statement: 'I didn't think that this would ever happen to me.'

Other people believe in a kind of universal 'deservingness', where only bad things happen to those who deserve it. For example, when a mother loses her baby in a cot-death, she may well believe irrationally (but understandably): 'Because neither my young baby or anybody in my family has done anything to deserve this, it therefore absolutely should not have happened.'

When such tragic events do happen to religious people, they either give up their faith, or their belief in God is severly tested because they believe, again irrationally, that: 'God absolutely should not have allowed such a tragedy to happen.' Rabbi Harold Kushner (1982) has written an interesting book, entitled 'When Bad Things Happen to Good People', which deals with this issue more fully.

Rational-emotive psychology keenly distinguishes between catastrophes and tragedies on the one hand, and the concept of 'awfulising' on the other (see Chapter 4 for a fuller discussion of awfulising). REP acknowledges that such tragedies and catastrophes do happen in life and recognise that it is very easy for most people to awfulise about them. Such awfulising, according to Albert Ellis, is derived from a musturbatory belief, e.g. 'This tragedy absolutely should not have occurred and it is awful that it did.' Contrast this with the rational alternative 'I would much prefer it if this tragedy did not exist, but unfortunately there is no reason why it absolutely should not have happened. It is tragic, but not the end of the world.' This latter belief reflects the REP viewpoint that 'tragedies are not awful, but they are tragic'. I want to stress that this is not playing with words. If you have followed the argument outlined in this book, particularly in Chapter 4, you will appreciate that this viewpoint represents a serious attempt to encourage people to be healthily distressed about tragedies without adding unhealthy emotional disturbance to these adversities.

I also want to stress that the variable of time often interacts with highly aversive actual A's and beliefs. While most people will think irrationally about the occurrence of actual tragedies in their lives when these events have just happened, the majority of these people will eventually think rationally about these actual A's, although it may take some of them years to be able to do so.*

Some people unfortunately never stop thinking irrationally about such tragedies and live miserable lives as a result because they constantly think about the tragedy, while others are able to push such events out of their mind even though they still hold underlying irrational beliefs about the occurrences.**

A small minority of people are able to think rationally about tragedies even at the point of their occurrence. A well known example is that of Gordon Wilson, whose daughter, Marie, was killed in the

---

* What happens in the intervening time period that enables people to think rationally about such tragic events is beyond the scope of this book.

**Again a discussion of why some people can put such tragedies to the back of their mind while others cannot, even though both groups retain irrational beliefs about the events in question, is beyond the scope of this book.

Enniskillen bombing that was carried out by the IRA, and in which Gordon Wilson, himself, was injured. Right after this tragedy, Wilson said that he felt no malice towards the bombers, which from an REP perspective means that he held no anger-based irrationalities towards them. He claimed later that his belief in God enabled him to be malice-free. The question as to the role of religious belief in encouraging such an immediate rational response to tragedy is one that merits scientific study.

A person's beliefs can also influence the actual events that to which a person pays attention. I have already made this point when showing the impact of inferred A's on actual A's (see p.116). For example, if a person believes irrationally that he or she is worthless because of failure to gain promotion at work, then he or she will pay attention to actual instances of people pointing out his or her job deficiencies and fail to register actual instances of people pointing out the job strengths. However, if the person believes rationally that he or she is a fallible human being, even though he or she failed to obtain promotion, then that person will pay attention to both types of actual A's.

Reciprocal influence III: how inferred A's influence and are influenced by B's and behavioural C's

You will recall that inferences are hunches about reality which go beyond the data at hand and relate to matters of personal significance within the individual's personal domain. In this section, I will consider how inferences are reciprocally related to beliefs and behaviours.

Inferred A's and B's

When inferred A's are negatively distorted they often (but not always) (1) stem from a person's irrational belief, and (2) trigger a further irrational belief. This can best be illustrated in the development of a panic attack where inferences and irrational beliefs interact at lightening speed to create mounting panic. This is illustrated in Figure 8.1.

Inferences that are less negatively distorted tend to trigger a person's irrational beliefs less frequently than inferences that are highly distorted negatively. Thus, when a person infers that not only will he or she fail to be promoted, but that he or she will also be made redundant, that person is more likely to think irrationally about this inferred A than about a prediction (i.e. predictive inference) that he or she will fail simply to be promoted.

A number of years ago, I did an experiment with two colleagues that showed the impact of beliefs on inferences (Dryden, Ferguson &

Actual A:	Feeling tense
Inferred A:	I'm going to have trouble breathing.
Irrational Belief:	I must be able to breathe more easily.
Inferred A:	I'm getting more anxious. I'm going to choke.
Irrational Belief:	I must be able to control my breathing right now.
Inferred A:	I'm going to die.
Irrational belief:	I must not die in this fashion.
C:	Strong panic.

Figure 8.1. Reciprocal influence between inferred A's and irrational beliefs.

McTeague, 1989). We asked one group of subjects to imagine that they held an irrational belief about spiders (i.e. 'I must not see a spider and it would be terrible if I did see one.'), and second group that they held a rational belief about spiders (i.e. 'I would prefer not to see spider, but there is no reason why I must not see one. If I do see a spider, it would be bad, but not terrible.'). Then, we told them to imagine that they would be going into a room where a spider had been spotted and we asked them to answer a number of questions while holding to the belief that they were assigned. Here is a sample of the questions that we asked:

- How many spiders are there in the room?
- What is the size of the spider(s) ?
- In which direction is (are) the spider(s) moving: Towards you, away from you or in a random direction?

The results of this experiment showed that when subjects held an irrational belief about spiders, they estimated that there would be more spiders in the room, that the spiders would be larger and that the spiders were more likely to be moving towards them, than for those subjects who held a rational belief about spiders. This suggests that holding an irrational belief leads people to make more highly distorted negative inferences than holding a rational belief.

Interestingly enough, the differential effect of beliefs on inferences that were found in the spider experiment was accentuated when subjects were asked to imagine that they would be entering a dark room alone, and attenuated when they were asked to imagine that they would be entering a light room accompanied by a friend. This demonstrates the important role that actual A's play in either exaggerating or minimizing the effect of beliefs on inferences.

Inferred A's and behavioural C's

When a person makes an inference about reality, he or she influences the way in which he or she tends to act (i.e. the action tendency) and the actual behaviour. This influence will be independent of his or her beliefs although, of course, beliefs will also play an important role here. Let me give an obvious example. Suppose you are walking alone at night down a dimly lit street and you hear a noise. Suppose you make the following inference; 'I am about to be mugged'. Whether you think rationally or irrationally about this you will have a tendency to take flight, to freeze or to turn and fight. Certainly, if you hold an irrational belief about your inference you will increase your chances of reacting in one of these three ways. But, even if you hold a rational belief about the prospect of being mugged, you will still tend to take flight, freeze or fight.

Conversely, if a person's acts in a certain way, his behaviour will have an influence on the inferences he makes. For example, if a person is at a party and approaches people, she is more likely to infer that these people are interested in talking to her than if she does not approach people.*

If the person does not approach people at the party, her lack of action on this occasion will prompt her to make inferences such as: 'They don't find me interesting. If they did, they would come up to talk to me', 'I don't have anything interesting to say to them. Since if I did, I would go up to talk to them', and 'They all know each other. They look on me as an outsider'. Of course, she would be more likely to make such inferences if she held irrational beliefs as opposed to rational beliefs in this situation. However, if her beliefs are taken out of the picture, her action (of initiating conversation with others) is more likely to

---

*This will not necessarily be the case if she holds an irrational belief such as 'I must entertain others and it is terrible if I do not', since she will think that others will find her boring if she does not entertain them sufficiently.

lead her to make positive inferences about others' reaction to her than her lack of action.

While taking action in this situation will in itself decrease the chances that the person will make negative inferences about others' reactions to her, such action provides her with direct feedback from others which, in most cases, contradicts any negative inferences that she might be making about the situation.*

However, if the person is inactive and does not initiate any conversation with others she does not get direct feedback from them to contradict her negative inferences. So, she is left with making inferences about why they have not approached her. In such a situation she is more likely to conclude that the reason they are not approaching her is because they do not find her interesting rather than the equally or more plausible inferential alternatives such as 'They are not approaching me because I am not approaching them,' or 'Maybe they think that I don't want to approach them, that's why they are not coming up to me'.

Reciprocal influence IV: how beliefs influence and are influenced by emotional and behavioural C's.

I have already considered in this chapter, the relationship between a person's beliefs and (a) the actual A's she encounters, (b) the inferences she makes and (c) the goals she has. In Chapters 5 and 6 respectively, I discussed the impact of holding rational and irrational beliefs on the emotions a person experiences, on the one hand and her action tendencies and actual behaviours on the other. Here, I will look at the impact of emotional and behavioural C's on the beliefs a person holds.

1. The impact of emotions on beliefs

While one of the principal tenets of rational-emotive psychology stresses the central role that beliefs play in determining a person's emotions, it is also the case that REP recognises that emotions can influence the beliefs that the person's holds. For example, if a person is depressed then he is more likely to think of himself as worthless than if he is sad, but not depressed. This is obviously the case when his original depression stems from ideas of worthlessness, but it is also likely to happen when his depression stems from other belief such as self-pity or other-

---

*Again I want to stress that if the person holds an irrational belief in this situation such as 'I must be entertaining', then she will be more likely to distort such feedback in a negative direction (e.g 'You see they did find me boring. They only laughed a little at my jokes').

pity ideas. This effect may well be mediated by beliefs, as when the person believes: 'I must not feel sorry for myself and I am worthless if I do. However, this influence of emotions on beliefs may occur in a less direct way. It is well known that when a person is depressed, he will tend to think more about negative actual or inferred A's than when he is sad, but not depressed. Thus, if the person is depressed about failing something important, he will tend to retrieve more past failures (actual or inferred) from his memory than when he is sad. Having thus retrieved these failure experiences from his memory, the person can do one of two things. First, he can reinforce his already activated irrational belief and second, he can use such evidence to create a new irrational belief.

In the first situation, the person focusses on the failure experiences that his depression has helped to retrieve from his memory and uses these as evidence to support his already activated irrational belief (i.e. 'I absolutely shouldn't have failed at this task and I am a failure for doing so. Not only that, but look at how many times I have failed in the past. This doubly proves what a failure I am').

Alternatively, in the second case, the retrieval of these past actual or inferred failures triggers a new irrational belief in the person. Having focussed on some of his past failures, the person then creates the following irrationality: 'I now see that I have failed at quite a few things in my life. I absolutely should not have failed so much in life'.

Conversely, when the person is sad but not depressed about a present failure, he will tend to think of both past failures and past successes. When he does focus on past failures, he will less likely create an irrational belief about these failures when he is sad than when he is depressed.

2. The impact of behaviours on beliefs

In Chapter 3, I showed how holding irrational beliefs influences the person to act in an unconstructive, self-defeating manner, while holding rational beliefs tends to promote more constructive, self-enhancing behaviour. As elsewhere, the relationship between beliefs and behaviour is reciprocal and behaviour can serve to reinforce existing beliefs or help trigger new ones.

For example, if a person holds an irrational belief that she is worthless and consequently withdraws from other people and sits for long periods alone in a darkened room, then she will more likely reinforce this belief than she would if she sought out company or engaged in an involving activity while alone. Similarly, if a person, while not depressed, sat alone in a darkened room, read only newspaper reports that detailed man's humanity to man and cut off contact with the outside world, then she is more likely to create irrational, depression-related beliefs than she would if she sat in a bright room, read newspaper reports dealing with good and bad news and responded to or initiated contact with other people.

Reciprocal influence V: how emotional C's influence and are influenced by actual A's and inferred A's

In Chapter 7, I discussed the impact of emotions on a person's action tendencies. Earlier in this chapter, I considered how emotions are reciprocally related to a person's goals and beliefs, Here, I look at the interrelations between emotions, on the one hand, and actual A's and inferred A's, on the other.

1. Emotions and actual A's

I have already noted that when a person encounters a highly aversive actual A, he is more likely to hold irrational beliefs about than if he encounters a lesser actual adversity. It follows from this that the person will more likely experience unhealthy negative emotions about highly negative actual A's than about less negative one's.

As I discussed in Chapter 7, and as I will soon underscore, different unhealthy negative emotions are associated with different inferences. This, of course, is particularly the case when the person concerned holds irrational beliefs about the inference. However, a person's inferences (which you will recall are hunches about reality) may be an accurate reflection about an actual A. In this sense then different actual A's, when they are actual embodiments of an inference pattern, are associated with different unhealthy negative emotions, again when the person thinks irrationally about the actual event.

Putting these two principles together – namely, (a) that a person is more likely to experience an unhealthy negative emotion about a highly aversive actual A than about a less aversive actual event and (b) that when actual A's embody inferences, then the person will experience different unhealthy negative emotions about different actual A's when he thinks irrationally about them – we arrive at the following. A person will be more likely to experience different unhealthy negative emotions when he encounters actual A's which embody different types of inferences when these actual A's are highly aversive than when they are moderately or mildly aversive.

For example, when a person experiences an actual loss, he will be more likely to depressed about it when the loss is a serious one than when it is less serious. Additionally, when a person encounters an actual threat, he will more likely be anxious about it if the threat is great than if it is less great. Of course, these statements hold true when the person's beliefs are taken out of the picture. When we bring them back into the picture then they can either protect the person against unhealthy negative emotions or make it more likely that he will experience them. Thus, if a person holds a rational belief about a serious loss, he will be less likely to experience depression than if he holds an irrational belief about a less serious loss.

When we consider the effect of emotions on Actual A's, we need to bear in mind that behaviour often serves as a mediating variable here. Thus, as shown in Chapter 7, when a person experiences an emotion she has a tendency to act in a certain way. If she then actualises this tendency and behaves in a certain manner she may, through her behaviour, encounter certain actual A's that she might not encounter if she did not act in that certain manner. Take, for example, a person who experiences anger towards a work colleague for threatening his self-esteem. When he is angry he has, you will recall from Chapter 7, a tendency to attack the source of this threat. Now, if he actualises this tendency he may encounter one or more of the following actual A's:

1. He may have a fight with his co-worker.
2. He may be disciplined for his unruly behaviour.
3. He may be fired for his aggression.
  and
4. He may get into trouble with the police as a result of the attack.

If he was annoyed but not angry about the inferred threat to his self-esteem, then he will have a different action tendency, which if actualised, will lead him to encounter a different set of actual A's. Thus, his annoyance will lead him to assert himself with his co-worker in a constructive way which may well lead to better relations between them. Now, it is true that if the person is angry, he does not have to actualise his action tendency and attack the other person. However, he is more likely to attack his work colleague when he is angry than when he is annoyed and consequently his anger increases the chances that he will encounter one or more of the illustrative actual A's listed above.

2. Emotions and inferred A's

I discussed in Chapter 7, the influence that inferred A's have on a person's emotions. Specifically, I showed that different inferences (or inferred A's) are associated with different healthy negative emotions (when the person holds a set of rational beliefs about the inferred A) and with different unhealthy emotions (when the person holds a set of irrational beliefs about the inferred A). I refer the reader back to Chapter 7 for a full discussion of this point.

Conversely, the way a person feels can influence the inferences that he makes about a given situation. Thus, if a person is already anxious, his anxiety will increase the likelihood that he will make threat-related inferences about the situation that he is in than if he is experiencing concern, but not anxiety. Also when he is in a situation that contain both threatening and non-threatening aspects, he is more likely to focus on the threatening features of the environment when he is already anxious than when he is already concerned.

As a further example if a person is already in a depressed state of mind he is more likely to make inferences about his past, present and future that relate to failure than he would if he is already experiencing sadness, but not depression.

Reciprocal influence VI: how behaviour influences and is influenced by A's, C's and G's

I have already covered in this chapter most of the interrelationships between behaviour and the other elements deemed important by rational-emotive psychology for a full understanding of how we function as humans. Thus, I have considered the ways in which behaviour has a reciprocal relationship with goals (see pp. 114–115), with inferred A's (see pp. 120–121) and with beliefs (see pp. 122–123). In the previous section, I showed how behaviour based on emotion can influence the kind of actual A's a person may encounter (see pp.123–124) and by showing the impact of actual A's on emotion (see pp. 123–124), I have alluded to the types of action tendencies a person may have in such situations. By extrapolating from action tendencies to behaviour, you can thus see how people may act under such circumstances.

This just leaves the relationship between behaviour and emotion. In Chapter 7, I discussed fully the types of action tendencies that are based on different healthy and unhealthy negative emotions. Thus, I have already shown the impact that emotions have on the ways in which a person tends to act. To bring this chapter to a close I discuss briefly the influence of behaviour on emotion.

1. The impact of behaviour on emotion

The ways in which behaviour can influence emotion can best be seen in situations where a person already experiences an unhealthy negative emotion. Basically, when a person experiences such an emotion, the more he actualises the action tendency on which that emotion is based, the more he will perpetuate that emotion in the longer term. However, the more he actualises the action tendency associated with the relevant healthy negative alternative, the more chance he has of changing his unhealthy negative emotion to that healthy alternative.

Take anxiety, for example. If a person is anxious and withdraws from the situation (action tendency), then although he will experience an immediate reduction in anxiety, he increases the chances that he will become anxious in the same or similar situations in the future. This is because by withdrawing, the person has reinforced his irrational beliefs that underpinned his anxiety in the first place. If the person is to deal with his anxiety productively, he needs to remain in the situation and tolerate his anxious feelings until he experiences healthy concern. In this case the person's behaviour has allowed him to remain in the situation where he can challenge and change his anxiety-based irrational beliefs, thus enabling him to experience the more healthy emotion of concern.

This marks the end of the book. I hope that you have enjoyed this invitation to rational-emotive psychology. If you would like to know more about this approach to psychology and its therapeutic applications I have prepared a brief guide to further reading which now follows.

Suggestions for further reading

Bernard, M. & DiGiuseppe, R. (1989). *Inside rational-emotive therapy*. New York: Academic Press.
This book is a compilation of chapters on various aspects of rational-emotive psychology and its therapeutic applications, and is written by outside authorities. Of particular interest to readers of this book are chapters on REP-related philosophy and personality theory and the stance on the relationship between thoughts and feelings. In the closing chapter, Albert Ellis responds to his critics.

Dryden, W. & Yankura, J. (1993). *Counselling individuals: A rational-emotive handbook*. London: Whurr Publishers.
This book is a thorough introduction to the therapeutic applications of rational-emotive psychology with special reference to counselling individuals. It contains a first-hand account of this approach to therapy, written by a client.

Dryden, W. & Yankura, J. (1992). *Daring to be myself: A case of rational-emotive therapy*. Buckingham: Open University Press.
Unique in the annals of psychotherapy, this book contains extensive verbatim transcripts of a therapy conducted by Windy Dryden with the client, 'Sarah'. It also contains interviews with both client and therapist conducted 8 years after the end of therapy, which shows the long-term effects that can be achieved from a relatively brief intervention if the client applies what he or she learns about REP.

Yankura, J. & Dryden, W. (1994). *Albert Ellis*. London: Sage.
Looking at the life and work of Albert Ellis, this book opens with a biographical chapter and then considers the theoretical and practical contributions that Albert Ellis has made to the field of psychotherapy. There follows a detailed evaluation of criticisms of Ellis's work and the formulation of appropriate rebuttals. The book finishes with an overall

assessment of the importance of Ellis's work to the field of psychotherapy.

Scholarly articles on rational emotive behaviour therapy are regularly published in the *Journal of Rational-Emotive and Cognitive Behavior Therapy*, published by Human Sciences Press.

References

Beck, A.T. (1976). *Cognitive Therapy and the Emotional Disorders*. New York: International Universities Press.

DiGiuseppe, R. (1988). Thinking what to feel. In W. Dryden & P. Trower (Eds), *Developments in Rational-Emotive Therapy*. Milton Keynes: Open University Press.

Dryden, W. (1986). Language and meaning in rational-emotive therapy. *Journal of Rational-Emotive Therapy* 4(2), 131–142.

Dryden, W. (1990). *Dealing with Anger Problems: Rational-Emotive Therapeutic Interventions*. Sarasota, FL: Professional Resource Exchange.

Dryden, W. (1992). *The Incredible Sulk*. London: Sheldon.

Dryden, W. (1994). *Overcoming Guilt*. London: Sheldon.

Dryden, W., Ferguson, J., & McTeague, S. (1989). Beliefs and inferences: A test of a rational-emotive hypothesis. 2: On the prospect of seeing a spider. *Psychological Reports* 64, 115–123.

Ellis, A. (1958). Rational psychotherapy. *Journal of General Psychology* 59, 35–49.

Ellis, A. (1978). Toward a theory of personality. In R.J. Corsini (Ed.), *Readings in Current Personality Theories*. Itasca, IL: Peacock.

Ellis, A. (1979). Discomfort anxiety: A new cognitive behavioral construct. Part 1. *Rational Living* 14(2), 3–8.

Ellis, A. (1980). Discomfort anxiety: A new cognitive behavioral construct. Part 2. *Rational Living* 15(1), 25–30.

Ellis, A. (1983). 'The case against religiosity'. New York: Institute for Rational-Emotive Therapy.

Ellis, A. (1990). *How to Stubbornly Refuse to Make Yourself Miserable About Anything – Yes, Anything*. Secaucus, NJ: Lyle Stuart.

Ellis, A. (1991). The revised ABCs of RET. *Journal of Rational-Emotive and Cognitive Behavior Therapy* 9, 139–72.

Hauck, P. (1971). A RET theory of depression. *Rational Living* 6(2), 32–35.

Kushner, H.S. (1982). *When Bad Things Happen to Good People*. London: Pan.

Weinrach, S. (1980). Unconventional therapist: Albert Ellis. *Personnel and Guidance Journal* 59, 152–160.

Index

A causes C model, 39-40, 44
ABC framework, 7-8
   activating events, 9-16
   beliefs, 17-37
   driving test example, 51-52
   heartache example, 39-44
   interactions within, 111-126
   reunion example, 58, 60
absolutism, irrational beliefs, 6, 21, 24, 27
abstraction levels of beliefs, 32-37
acceptance beliefs, 27-30
action tendencies, 77-79
   anger/annoyance, 89, 90
   anxiety/concern, 82-83, 84
   depression/sadness, 85-86, 87
   envy, healthy and unhealthy, 106, 107
   guilt/remorse, 92, 93
   hurt/disappointment, 99-100, 101
   jealousy/concern for relationships, 102-103, 104
   shame/regret, 95-96, 97-98
activating events (A's), 8, 9-16, 17
   emotional responsibility, 45
   and emotions, 52, 58, 60
   heartache example, 39, 41, 42, 43
   reciprocal influences, 112, 115-121
actual activating events, 10-11, 17
   and beliefs, 13, 14, 15-16, 18
   and critical activating events, 13
   heartache example, 42
   reciprocal influences, 112, 115-118, 123-124
aggressive sulking, 99
anger, 87-89

action tendencies, 78, 79
   'false', 61
   about guilt, 108-109
   and hurt, 99-100
   reciprocal influences, 124
   reunion example, 57, 58
annoyance, 59, 70, 90, 124
anorgasmia, 70
anti-awfulising beliefs, 23-24
anxiety, 81-83
   driving test example, 51-53, 54-56
   meta-emotional problems, 109-110
   reciprocal influences, 126
   reunion example, 57, 58-59
   self-esteem, 82, 88
   termination, 66
assertiveness, 78-79
auto-erotic asphyxia, 71
aversive emotions, 53
avoidance of emotional state, 67-68, 83
awfulising beliefs, 22, 24-25, 117

Beck, Aaron T., 12, 13
behaviour, 4, 5, 17, 63-80
   anger/annoyance, 89, 90
   anxiety/concern, 82, 84
   depression/sadness, 85, 86-87
   envy, healthy and unhealthy, 105-106, 107
   guilt/remorse, 91-92, 93
   hurt/disappointment, 99, 101
   jealousy/concern for relationship, 102, 103-104
   reciprocal influences, 114-115, 120-121, 122-123, 125-126
   shame/regret, 95, 97

Index

behavioural competence, 79-80
beliefs (B's), 8, 17-37
   activating events, 13-16
   behavioural competence, 80
   heartache example, 41, 42-44
   rape example, 49
   reciprocal influences, 112-113, 116-120, 121-123
   see also irrational beliefs; rational beliefs
Bernard, M., 127
blaming the victim, 45-46
boredom, 64, 66
broad activating events, 9

chaining of activating events and beliefs, 13-16, 18
cognitions see behaviour
cognitive therapy, 12
commission, acts of, 91, 93, 98
compensatory behaviour, 79
competence, behavioural, 79-80
concern, 83-84
   driving test example, 52, 53, 54-56
   for relationship, 103-104
   reunion example, 59, 60
condemning beliefs, 30-31
condonement of deficiencies, 29-30
consequences (C's), 8
   activating events, 13
   heartache example, 39, 41, 42, 43
   see also behaviour; emotions
consistency with reality, rational beliefs, 6, 21, 23-24, 26, 29
constructive negative emotions, 6, 51-56, 59-60
   action tendencies, 78-79
conviction of beliefs, 54, 56
core beliefs, 34-35
critical activating events, 13, 16
   and beliefs, 18
   emotions, 60
   heartache example, 42

de Forrest, Izette, 3
defensive nature, irrational beliefs, 31-32
demanding anger, 87, 90
depression, 84-86, 99-100, 121-122

desiring beliefs, 20-21
   and acceptance beliefs, 27, 29
   and anti-awfulising beliefs, 23, 24
   and high frustration tolerance beliefs, 25, 26
   primacy, 22
development of rational-emotive psychology, 2-5
DiGiuseppe, Raymond, 61, 127
disappointment, 43-44, 46-47, 100-101
discomfort disturbance, 37
   anger, 88
   anxiety, 82, 83
   depression, 84, 86
downing beliefs, 30-32
driving test example, 51-57
drugs, 64, 71
Dryden, Windy, 24, 30, 87, 90, 118, 127
   sulking, 74, 75, 99

eating behaviour, 71-72, 92
ego disturbance, 37
   anger, 88-89
   anxiety, 82, 83
   depression, 84, 85, 86
elegant philosophies, 37
Ellis, Albert
   anxiety, 82
   awfulising and anti-awfulising beliefs, 23, 24, 117
   development of RET, 1, 2-5
   goals, 111
   low frustration tolerance beliefs, 26
   primacy of musts and preferences, 22, 23, 117
   psychological disturbance, 37
   specific beliefs, 33
embarrassment, 96
emotional responsibility, 44-50
emotions, 51-62
   A causes C model, 39-40
   and action tendencies, 77
   definition, 7
   and inferences, 10, 11, 12-13
   as internal activating events, 10
   and interpretations, 10
   rational therapy, 4, 5
   reciprocal influences, 113-114, 121-122, 123-126
envy, 101, 104-107
Epictetus, 3

Index

ethical principles, 91
evaluative beliefs, 17-18, 80
'evil eye' belief, 70
external activating events, 10
extremity
  awfulising beliefs, 23
  low frustration tolerance beliefs, 25, 27

'false' emotions, 60-62
Ferenczi, Sandor, 3
Ferguson, J., 118
flexibility, rational beliefs, 6, 20, 23, 25, 28-29
Forrest, Izette de, 3
free floating anxiety, 109
frustration, 87, 88
future activating events, 10

gambling, 74
general beliefs, 33-34, 35-37
goals (G's)
  achievement of, 6, 21, 24, 26 29
  long-term, 64, 76-77
  obstacles to, 7, 22, 25, 27
  reciprocal influences, 111-115
  short-term, 64
guilt, 90-92
  abut anger, 108-109
  'false', 61
  intensification, 71-72
  reunion example, 57, 58

Hankin-Wessler, Sheila, 64-65
Hauck, Paul, 85, 87
healthy envy, 106-109
heartache, 39-48
high frustration tolerance (HFT) beliefs, 25-26
hurt, 39-47, 98-100

illogicality, irrational beliefs, 6, 21-22, 24, 27
inconsistency with reality, irrational beliefs, 6-7, 22, 25, 27
indifference, 42, 56-57, 113
inferences, 17
  anger/annoyance, 87-88, 90
  anxiety/concern, 82, 83
  and beliefs, 13-16, 18
  core nature, 41

inferences (contd)
  as critical activating events, 13
  depression/sadness, 84, 86
  and emotions, 10, 52, 58-59
  envy, healthy and unhealthy, 104-105, 107
  guilt/remorse, 91, 93
  heartache example, 41, 42-43, 44
  hurt/disappointment, 98, 100-101
  and interpretations, 11-12
  jealousy/concern for relationships, 101, 103
  meta-emotional problems, 109
  and personal domain, 12-13
  reciprocal influences, 112, 115-116, 118-121, 124-125
  shame/regret, 94, 96
  skill levels, 80
initiation of emotional state, 64-66
intensity of emotions, 68-72
intermittently reinforced behaviour, 74
internal activating events, 10
internal experience of emotions, 53
interpersonal environment, response elicitation, 74-76
interpretations, 17
  and actual activating events, 11
  and beliefs, 13, 14, 15-16, 18
  and critical activating events, 13
  emotions as, 10
  and inferences, 11-12
irrational beliefs, 18, 19-31
  anger, 88-89
  anxiety, 82
  behavioural competence, 80
  characteristics, 6-7
  defensive nature, 31-32
  depression, 84-85
  envy, unhealthy, 105
  guilt, 91
  heartache example, 42, 43, 44
  hurt, 98
  jealousy, 101
  meta-emotional problems, 109
  philosophies, 35, 37
  purposive behaviour, 64, 69-70, 72, 73, 74
  shame, 94-95
  specificity, 33-34
  unconstructive negative emotions, 51-52, 54, 55-59

Index

jealousy, 101-103, 110

Kelly, Brian, 20
Kushner, H.S., 117

LAMP Institute, 2-3
life conditions, condemning/downing, 31, 32
logicality, rational beliefs, 6, 20-21, 23, 25-26, 29
long-term goals, 64, 76-77
low frustration tolerance (LFT) beliefs, 25, 26-27

maintenance of emotion, 72-73
'M*A*S*H' example, 14-16, 18
McTeague, S., 119
meta-emotional problems, 108-110
mixed emotions, 57-60
moral codes, 91, 92-93
musturbatory beliefs, 20, 21-22
    and awfulising beliefs, 24, 117
    and condemning/downing beliefs, 30, 31
    and emotions, 56, 57
    and low frustration tolerance beliefs, 26
    specificity, 33

negative emotions, 81
    action tendencies, 77
    avoidance, 67-68
    constructive, 6, 51-56, 59-60
    heartache example, 43-44
    initiation, 64-65
    intensification, 71-72
    maintenance, 72-73
    minimisation, 68-69
    response options, 78-79
    termination, 66
    unconstructive, 6, 51-59, 60, 61
non-demanding anger, 87, 90
non-verbal behaviour, 61

omission, acts of, 91, 93, 98
options, response, 78-79
other-condemning beliefs, 30-32

panic attacks, 68-69, 109, 118
past activating events, 9-10
personal domain, 12-13, 34, 87

personal rules, transgression of, 87-88
personal significance
    inferences, 11, 12-13, 14, 15, 18
    themes, 34-35, 36
philosophies, 35-37
physical environment, response elicitation, 73-74
positive emotions, 6
    initiation, 64
    intensification, 70-71
    maintenance, 72
    minimisation, 69-70
    termination, 67
pragmatism, rational beliefs, 6
preference statements, 20
preferential beliefs, 19-21
    and acceptance beliefs, 27, 29
    and anti-awfulising beliefs, 23, 24
    and high frustration tolerance beliefs, 25, 26
    primacy, 22
presently-occurring activating events, 9
primacy of musts and preferences, 22-23
procrastination, 67-68, 72-73
promotion example, 20-35, 111-115, 116, 118
psychological disturbance, 37
purposive nature of behaviour, 63-77

rape, 48-50, 115-116
rational beliefs, 18, 19-31
    action tendencies, 78
    annoyance, 90
    behavioural competence, 80
    characteristics, 6
    concern, 83
    constructive negative emotions, 51, 52, 54, 55-57, 59-60

    disappointment, 100
    envy, healthy, 106-107
    heartache example, 42, 43, 44
    philosophies, 35-36, 37
    purposive behaviour, 76-77
    regret, 96-97
    relationship, concern for, 103
    remorse, 92-93
    sadness, 86
    specificity, 34, 35

rational emotive behaviour therapy (REBT), 1, 5, 7
rational-emotive therapy (RET), 5
rational therapy (RT), 3-5
rationalism, 4, 5
reciprocal influences, 111-126
regret, 96-98
religion, 117, 118
remorse, 59-60, 92-93, 108
resignation to facts, 29
response options, 78-79
   anger/annoyance, 89, 90
   anxiety/concern, 82-83, 84
   depression/sadness, 85-86, 87
   envy, healthy and unhealthy, 106, 107
   guilt/remorse, 92, 93
   hurt/disappointment, 99-100, 101
   jealousy/concern for relationship, 102-103, 104
   shame/regret, 95-97, 97-98
reunion example, 57-60
rigidity, irrational beliefs, 6, 21, 24, 27

sadness, 86-87, 121-122
self-condemning beliefs, 30, 31-32
self-defeating actions, 77
self-esteem, threat to, 82, 88
self-protective actions, 77
shame, 93-96, 110

short-term goals, 64
silent sulking, 99
specific activating events, 9
specific beliefs, 32-33
spider experiment, 119-120
standards, behaviour consistent with, 76-77
sulking, 74-76, 99
super-elegant philosophies, 37
Suttie, Ian, 3

task-irrelevant thoughts, 53
task-relevant thoughts, 53
termination of emotional state, 66-67
time, effects of, 117
tragic activating events, 48-50

unconstructive negative emotions, 6, 51-59, 60, 61, 78
unhealthy envy, 104-106

values, behaviour consistent with, 76-77
verbal behaviour, 61

Weinrach, Steve, 37
Wessler, Richard, 64-65
Wilson, Gordon, 117-118

Yankura, J., 127